THE OLD TESTAMENT

FOR CHRISTIANS

# ENJOYING

# JESUS'S

# BIBLE

## JASON S. DEROUCHIE

CRUCIFORM ⅁⅁ PRESS

CruciformPress.com | info@CruciformPress.com

"This book will change the way you read the Old and the New Testaments. Beyond this, if you are a pastor or teacher, this book will change the way you preach and teach from the Old and the New Testaments. Thankfully, while Jason DeRouchie's ideas are big, the words and the chapters are not. I will joyfully wear out my copy."

**Tom Kelby**, President, Hands to the Plow Ministries; President, Table Fellowship Churches

"Jason DeRouchie's love of the Old Testament is contagious. He loves the Old Testament because it leads him to his Savior. Neglecting the Old Testament results in an impoverished understanding of the words and works of Christ. Even though the Old Testament's language, culture, and worldview can strike modern readers as foreign or arcane, DeRouchie demonstrates how the Old Testament can be both accessible and awe-inspiring. He does more than merely inform his readers; he seeks to inflame their hearts, beginning with the Law and all the Prophets. DeRouchie serves the global church by opening the treasures of the Old Testament, allowing them to illuminate the New Testament, exalt Jesus, and lead readers to greater faithfulness and deeper worship."

**Joe M. Allen III**, Assistant Professor of Missions, Midwestern Baptist Theological Seminary and Spurgeon College

"While Christians may confess that the first three-quarters of the Bible is 'breathed out by God' (2 Tim. 3:16) and bears witness about Jesus (John 5:39), and although they may affirm that it is 'profitable for teaching, for reproof, for correction, and for training in righteousness' (2 Tim. 3:16), they often find it difficult to discover in it the kinds of life-transforming riches that would lead them to be 'complete, equipped for every good work' (2 Tim. 3:17). Put another way, it is one thing to believe that the Old Testament is a bottomless mine of life-transforming gospel gold, and it is quite another to experience its riches as one mines deeply. With this book, Jason DeRouchie has handed us a tool for mining, helped us get started, and given us instructions so that we can dig deeply for the rest of our lives. *Enjoying Jesus's Bible* provides a model for Christ-saturated and biblically grounded reading of the Old Testament as Christian Scripture. Church groups and classrooms will be blessed as they learn how to read, see, hope, and live in light of the Christ-centered message of the first three-quarters of the Bible."

**Ian J. Vaillancourt,** Professor of Old Testament and Hebrew, Heritage Theological Seminary; author, *The Dawning of Redemption and Treasuring the Psalms*

"We love to tell the stories of the Old Testament to children but, sadly, often fail to rejoice in it for ourselves. In *Enjoying Jesus's Bible*, Jason DeRouchie helps us see Christ in this part of God's word, resulting in a joy-filled faith. I highly recommend this book to you, whether you are a Christian in the pew or a leader in the church. Don't rush through it. You will see the Old Testament Scriptures as you have never seen them before!"

**Conrad Mbewe,** Pastor, Kabwata Baptist Church, Lusaka, Zambia; Founding Chancellor, African Christian University

"When it comes to Old Testament studies, Jason DeRouchie is one of this generation's most trusted authors. In *Enjoying Jesus's Bible*, he brings his considerable gifts to bear as he walks the reader through how to read the Old Testament in light of the person and work of Christ. This accessible, reader-friendly volume will biblically inform and spiritually inspire all who read it. Whether you're a new believer or an established scholar, I highly recommend this book."

**Jason K. Allen,** President, Midwestern Baptist Theological Seminary and Spurgeon College

"*Enjoying Jesus's Bible* covers an incredible amount of ground when it comes to helping us understand and apply 'Jesus's only Bible.' Of particular import is how much more attention and care teachers and evangelists should take as we teach the Old Testament. All Christians stand to benefit immensely as they worship their way through this comprehensive and informative text. Feel your heart leap for joy as you see how Jesus heals you of your spiritual disabilities and purchases for you every spiritual blessing!"

**Gloria Furman,** author, *Labor with Hope* and *Missional Motherhood*

"Jason DeRouchie is a faithful guide to the Old Testament. He shows that its theological message is that God reigns, saves, and satisfies through covenant for his glory in Christ."

**Andy Naselli,** Professor of Systematic Theology and New Testament, Bethlehem College and Seminary; Elder, The North Church, Mounds View, Minnesota

"This book is a dream come true. For years, Jason DeRouchie has won my trust. He cherishes both the Hebrew Scriptures and the Messiah himself. And without pretense or fudging, he loves to see the genuine, authentic marriage of the sacred text and its supreme Treasure. Few take both the Old Testament and Christ with such seriousness and contagious joy. Now, in this book, a world-class professor leverages his learning and skill in the Hebrew language, discourse analysis, and the full text of Scripture to train lay leaders, common Christians, and all careful students of the Bible, not just to read and understand the Old Testament better, but through it to encounter the King himself in the full sweep of his majesty and to delight in him."

**David Mathis**, Senior Teacher and Executive Editor, desiringGod.org; Pastor, Cities Church, Saint Paul, Minnesota; author, *Habits of Grace*

"For a Christian, understanding how Jesus is the center and climax of Scripture is of utmost importance. In this volume, Jason DeRouchie channels decades of study to help readers appropriately read the Old Testament as Christian Scripture by examining how Jesus fulfills all of God's promises. I love this book because it helps believers delight in God's word and delight in the God who gave us his word."

**Benjamin L. Merkle**, M. O. Owens Jr. Chair of New Testament Studies and Research Professor of New Testament and Greek, Southeastern Baptist Theological Seminary; Editor, *Southeastern Theological Review*

"If delight is not the first word that comes to mind when you think about the Old Testament, then this book is a gift to you. Jason DeRouchie is a trusted scholar and just the man we need to teach us that the Old Testament prepares for and points to Jesus Christ. This happy discovery awaits all who read *Enjoying Jesus's Bible*."

**C. J. Mahaney**, Senior Pastor, Sovereign Grace Church, Louisville, Kentucky

"I have benefited from Jason DeRouchie's work both personally and professionally for decades, and this book represents yet another gift to those who would engage its content. His work is clear, thorough, and compelling. Additionally, his argument is fundamental and essential for the full and proper interpretation of the Old Testament as Christian Scripture. If you are not convinced, repent and reread it."

**Miles V. Van Pelt**, Alan Hayes Belcher, Jr. Professor of Old Testament and Biblical Languages and Director, Summer Institute for Biblical Languages, Reformed Theological Seminary, Jackson

"Jason DeRouchie's work will be immensely helpful to a wide variety of readers. It is both accessible and comprehensive. It is practical and well researched. I'm looking forward to hearing of its impact in a variety of contexts around the globe."

**Ryan Robertson**, President, Reaching & Teaching International Ministries; Elder, Third Avenue Baptist Church, Louisville, Kentucky

*To Gary Pratico, whose reverence for God
and whose joy in Jesus and his Bible
helped shape the man I am and am becoming*

# About the Author

Jason S. DeRouchie is Research Professor of Old Testament and Biblical Theology and the Rich and Judy Hastings Endowed Chair of Old Testament Studies at Midwestern Baptist Theological Seminary. He also serves as Content Developer and Global Trainer with Hands to the Plow Ministries and as a pastor of Sovereign Joy Baptist Church in the northland of Kansas City, MO. He and his wife, Teresa, have been married since 1994.

## CRUCIFORM ⓖ PRESS

We publish clear, useful, biblically faithful, and mostly short books for Christians and other curious people. Books that tackle serious subjects in a readable style. We do this because the good news of Jesus Christ—the gospel—is the only thing that actually explains why this world is so wonderful and so awful all at the same time. Even better, the gospel applies to every single area of life, and offers real answers that aren't available from any other source.

CruciformPress.com

*Enjoying Jesus's Bible: The Old Testament for Christians*

Print / PDF ISBN: 978-1-941114-77-3   ePub ISBN: 978-1-941114-78-0

# CONTENTS

# PREFACE

Three-fourths of our Christian Bible is *Old* Testament, and this was Jesus's only Scripture. God led the prophets of old to write it "for our instruction" and to serve us (Rom. 15:4; 1 Cor. 10:11; 1 Pet. 1:12). This little book seeks to equip Christian laypeople to delight in the reality that the Old Testament is *Christian* Scripture. It attempts to be immensely practical by addressing:

- *reading* the Old Testament the way God intends (chapter 1),
- *seeing* Jesus where Scripture discloses him (chapter 2),
- *hoping* in all God's promises for us (chapter 3), and
- *living* faithfully in relation to God's law (chapter 4).

In this accessible guide, you will discover how to make connections to Christ and practical application to the Christian life from every page of the Old Testament. Studying these texts within their close, continuing, and complete biblical contexts, you will see the books of the Old Testament the way God intends — as relevant parts of your Bible that God uses to make much of Christ and to help you live for him.

This book is an abridgement of my *Delighting in the Old Testament: Through Christ and for Christ* (Wheaton, IL: Crossway, 2024), and I thank Justin Taylor and Crossway for allowing me to publish this shorter work. I also thank my doctoral research assistant Brandon Benziger for helping me distill my larger book into short blog posts (ftc.co), and then I thank my research assistants Kaden Classen, Jonathan Lumley, and Jonathan Zavodney for copyediting help. I am grateful to publisher Kevin Meath and Cruciform Press for allowing me to rework these posts into this little book. I pray that it will help believers enjoy Jesus's Bible in increasing ways, all for the glory of Christ and the health of his church.

Two decades ago, I shared with John Piper and Justin Taylor my longing to help people revel in God's glory from the initial three-fourths of our Bible. When Pastor John asked for reflections, Justin said one sentence that changed the course of my life: "I hear a lot about the glory of God and very little about Jesus!" These words shook me to the core, and God used them and the following years of sitting under John Piper's preaching, partnering with him and an amazing faculty at Bethlehem College & Seminary, and serving as Sunday School teacher and elder of Bethlehem Baptist Church to reorient my affections and to set me on a path of discovery and awe that I am still walking today. This book contains some fruit of these years of growth.[1]

The author of Hebrews charged, "Remember your leaders, those who spoke to you the word of God. Consider the outcome of their way of life, and imitate their faith" (Heb. 13:7). I dedicate this book to Dr. Gary Pratico, whose humility, manhood, mentoring, teaching, counsel, and friendship have throughout my adult life reformed and renewed my own quest for joy in the Lord. From my graduate school days at Gordon-Conwell Theological Seminary through my formative wrestlings during my doctoral studies and across my more than two decades of academic and local church ministry, his faithfulness to and reverence for our holy God and his true and trustworthy Word have helped me love Jesus more as a man, husband, father, friend, professor, and pastor. Through such men we learn what it means to join those "who through faith and patience inherit the promises" (6:12). May God keep us faithful (13:20–21).

---

1. To overview this part of my story, see Jason S. DeRouchie, "When My Old Testament Became Christian," DesiringGod, Aug 7, 2024: https://www.desiringgod.org/articles/when-my-old-testament-became-christian.

# Does the Old Testament Really Matter for Christians?

*For whatever was written in former days was written
for our instruction. (Rom. 15:4)*

Is Christ really part of the Old Testament? Should I as a believer in the twenty-first century claim Old Testament promises as mine? Does the Mosaic law still matter today for followers of Jesus? Is the Old Testament *Christian* Scripture, and if so, how should this impact our understanding and application?

This book seeks to help Christians make connections to Christ and practical application to the Christian life from every page of the Old Testament. More specifically, it seeks to help you:

- by *faith* see and celebrate Christ in the Old Testament in faithful ways,
- rightly *hope* in Old Testament promises through Jesus, and
- genuinely *love* others with the help of the old-covenant law and its fulfillment in Jesus.

To understand the Old Testament fully, we must read it as believers in Jesus, with God having awakened our spiritual senses to see and hear rightly. That is, we read *through Christ.*

Then, as Christians, biblical interpretation reaches its end only after we have found Jesus and experienced him transforming us into his image. We, thus, read *for Christ*.

Some Christians may query, "If we are part of the new covenant, why should we seek to understand and apply the Old Testament?" While I will develop my response throughout this book, what follows are ten reasons why the Old Testament matters for Christians and why "Old" does not imply "unimportant" or "insignificant."

# 1. The Old Testament Was Jesus's Only Bible and Comprises 75% of Christian Scripture

If space says anything, the Old Testament matters to God, who gave us his word in a Book. In fact, it was his first special revelation, and it set a foundation for the fulfillment we find in Jesus in the New Testament. The Old Testament was the only Bible of Jesus and the earliest church (e.g., Luke 24:44; Acts 24:14), and it is a major part of our Scriptures.

# 2. The Old Testament Influences Our Understanding of Key Biblical Teachings

Without the Old Testament, we wouldn't understand the problem for which Jesus and the New Testament supply the solution (Rom. 5:18). We would miss so many features of God's salvation story (9:4–5). And we wouldn't grasp the various types and shadows that point to Jesus (John 1:29; 2:19, 21). Furthermore, some teachings, such as the doctrine of creation, are best understood from the Old Testament (Gen. 1:1–2:3). Finally, the New Testament worldview and teachings are built upon the framework supplied in the Old Testament.

## 3. We Meet the Same God in Both Testaments

Note how the book of Hebrews begins: "Long ago, at many times and in many ways, God spoke to our fathers by the prophets, but in these last days he has spoken to us by his Son" (Heb. 1:1–2). The very God who spoke through Old Testament prophets speaks through Jesus!

But isn't the Old Testament's God one of wrath, whereas the God of the New Testament is about grace? Not exactly. Indeed, both the Old and New Testaments indicate that the true and living God is one of both grace and wrath (e.g., Exod. 34:6–7; Matt. 10:28–31; Rev. 19). We meet the same God in the Old Testament as we do in the New.

## 4. The Old Testament Announces the Very "Good News" We Enjoy

Paul stresses that the Lord "promised beforehand through his prophets in the holy Scriptures" the very powerful "gospel of God ... concerning his Son" (Rom. 1:1–3; cf. Gal. 3:8). Foremost among these prophets was Isaiah, who anticipated the day when Yahweh's royal Servant (the Messiah) would herald comforting "good news" to the poor and broken (Isa. 61:1; cf. 40:9–11; 52:7–10; Luke 4:16–21). Reading the Old Testament, therefore, is one of God's given ways for us to better grasp and delight in the gospel (see also Heb. 4:2).

## 5. Both Testaments Call Us to Love and Clarify What Love Looks Like

As with Israel, the Lord calls Christians to lives characterized by love (Deut. 6:5; 10:19; Matt. 22:37–40; cf. Matt. 7:12; Rom. 13:8, 10; Gal. 5:14). However, he now gives all members of the new covenant the ability to do what he commands. As Moses himself asserted, the old-covenant law called for life-encompassing love (Deut. 30:6), and Christians today can gain clarity from the Old Testament on the wide-ranging impact of love in all of life. As we will see, this happens rightly only when we account for how Jesus fulfills every old-covenant law.

## 6. Jesus Came Not to Set Aside the Old Testament but to Fulfill It

Far from setting aside the Old Testament, Jesus stressed that he came to fulfill it, and he highlighted how the Old Testament's instruction was lastingly relevant for his followers (Matt. 5:17–19). In chapter four we'll consider further the significance of this text, but what is important to note here is that, while the age of the old covenant has come to an end (Rom. 6:14–15; 1 Cor. 9:20–21; Gal. 5:18; cf. Luke 16:16), the Old Testament itself maintains relevance for us in the way it (a) displays the character of God (e.g., Rom. 7:12), (b) points to the excellencies of Christ, and (c) portrays for us the scope of love in all its facets (Matt. 22:37–40).

# 7. Jesus Said That All the Old Testament Points to Him

Jesus himself said, "You search the Scriptures because you think that in them you have eternal life; and it is they that bear witness about me" (John 5:39; cf. 1:45; 5:46–47). Then, following his resurrection, he opened his disciples' minds "to understand the Scriptures, and said to them, 'Thus it is written that the Christ should suffer and on the third day rise from the dead, and that repentance and forgiveness of sins should be proclaimed in his name to all nations, beginning from Jerusalem" (Luke 24:45–47; cf. 24:27; Acts 26:22–23; 1 Cor. 2:2). A proper "understanding" of the Old Testament will lead one to hear in it a message of a suffering and resurrected Messiah and the mission his life would generate.

# 8. The New Testament Authors Expect Us to Read the Old Testament

The New Testament often cites the Old Testament in ways that call us back to look at the original context. For example, Matthew 27–28 portray Christ's tribulation and triumph at the cross by recalling Psalm 22 many times. Jesus quotes Psalm 22:1 when he declares, "My God, my God, why have you forsaken me?" (Matt. 27:46). In stating, "And when they had crucified him, they divided his garments among them by casting lots" (Matt. 27:35), Matthew alludes to Psalm 22:16, 18, which reads: "They have pierced my hands and feet.... They divide my garments among them, and for my clothing they cast lots." To fully understand their words, the New Testament authors call us back to the Old Testament through their quotations and allusions.

## 9. The New Testament Authors Recognized That God Gave the Old Testament for Christians

Regarding the Old Testament prophets, Peter indicates, "It was revealed to them that they were serving not themselves but you" (1 Pet. 1:12). Similarly, Paul was convinced that the Old Testament authors wrote *for* new-covenant believers—those following Jesus on this side of his death and resurrection. "For whatever was written in former days was written *for our instruction*, that through endurance and through the encouragement of the Scriptures we might have hope" (Rom. 15:4; cf. 4:23–24; 1 Cor. 10:11).

## 10. Paul Demands That Church Leaders Preach the Old Testament

Significantly, Paul was referring to the Old Testament when he spoke of the "sacred writings" that are able to make a person "wise for salvation" and of the "Scripture" that is "breathed out by God and profitable" (2 Tim. 3:15–16). Knowing this fact colors our understanding of his charge in 2 Timothy 4:2–4. In short, Paul believed Christians like Timothy needed to preach the Old Testament to guard the church from apostasy. While we now have the New Testament, we still must study, practice, and teach the Old Testament like Jesus and his apostles did for the good of God's church.

# Conclusion

*Enjoying Jesus's Bible* seeks to supply believers with an interpretive framework and guide for rightly handling the Old Testament as God's Word for Christians (2 Tim. 2:15–17). It approaches the Old Testament *through Christ and for Christ.* The book gives one chapter to each of four important questions that relate to different spheres of the Christian life. Because all the Bible is God's Word and the believer's authoritative guide for faith and practice, chapter 1 guides Christians in *reading well* and seeks to answer, "How can Jesus help Christians interpret the Old Testament?" Chapter 2 addresses *seeing well* as God intends and responds to the query, "How does Jesus's Bible testify about him?" Chapter 3 covers *hoping well* in God's promises and answers, "How does Jesus secure every divine promise?" Finally, chapter 4 tackles *living well* in alignment with God's instructions and considers, "How does Jesus make Moses's law matter?" Keep reading to enjoy Jesus's Bible better!

# One

# Reading Well

## How Does Jesus Help Christians Interpret the Old Testament?

*Concerning this salvation, the prophets ... prophesied
about the grace that was to be yours....
It was revealed to them that they were serving not
themselves but you. (1 Pet. 1:10, 12)*

The Old Testament has always been Christian Scripture—a collection of sacred, authoritative texts written for Christians to portray God's greatness and to instill hope in Christ. The Old and New Testaments agree that God originally gave the Old Testament with Christians in mind and that the Old Testament authors themselves recognized what they wrote would be more meaningful for those living in the messianic age of restoration than for those living before it, whether believer or nonbeliever. Furthermore, faith in Christ alone supplies the necessary light for seeing and savoring God's revelation in Jesus's Bible, and Jesus's appearing in salvation history supplies the necessary lens for most fully understanding and appropriating God's intended meaning in the Old Testament.

# New Testament Reflections on Grasping the Old Testament's Message

## For Whom Was the Old Testament Written?

According to the New Testament authors, the Old Testament authors knew that they were speaking and writing for new-covenant believers, and they also had some level of conscious awareness about who the Christ would be and when he would rise. With Christ's coming, anticipation gives rise to fulfillment and shadows turn to substance, which means that new-covenant members can comprehend the fullness of the Old Testament's meaning better than the old-covenant rebel and remnant.

Romans 4:23–24, 15:4, and 1 Corinthians 10:11 stress that the Old Testament authors wrote their texts for the benefit of believers living this side of the cross. For Paul, the Old Testament *is* Christian Scripture that does not reach its intended end until fully applied through Christ to the Christian's life.

The apostle said this much to Timothy as well. Speaking about the Jewish Scriptures, he wrote that the "sacred writings ... are able to make you wise for salvation through faith in Christ Jesus" (2 Tim. 3:15). Thus, Paul asserts, "All Scripture is ... profitable for teaching, for reproof, for correction, and for training in righteousness, that the man of God may be competent, equipped for every good work" (3:16–17).

Based on this fact, New Testament authors frequently cite Old Testament instructions, assuming their relevance for believers today. For example, Paul reaches into the Ten Commandments when addressing children (Eph. 6:2–3; cf. Exod. 20:12; Deut. 5:16) and draws on execution texts from Deuteronomy when speaking about excommunication (1 Cor. 5:13;

cf. Deut. 22:21, 22, 24). Peter also recalls the refrain from Leviticus when he writes, "Be holy in all your conduct, since it is written, 'You shall be holy, for I am holy'" (1 Pet. 1:15–16; cf. Lev. 11:44–45; 19:2; 20:26). Because we are now part of the new covenant and not the old, there are natural questions that rise regarding how exactly the Christian should relate to specific old-covenant promises or laws (see chapters three and four on these topics). Nevertheless, the point stands that God gave the Old Testament for Christian instruction.

Paul was not explicit as to whether it was only God's intent, as the ultimate author, to write the Old Testament for our instruction, or whether this was also the human authors' intent. Peter, however, made this clear when he wrote that "it was revealed to [the Old Testament prophets] that they were serving not themselves but you" (1 Pet. 1:12). He emphasized that the human authors themselves knew that their Old Testament words were principally *not for themselves* but for those living after the arrival of the Christ. Therefore, the Old Testament is more *relevant* for Christians today than it was for those in the old-covenant era.

## The Old Testament Prophets' Understanding of Christ's Person and Time

In John 8:56, Jesus declared that Abraham eagerly expected the coming of the Messiah. Similarly, Peter believed that David himself anticipated Christ's coming in Psalm 16 (Acts 2:30–31), and David's last words affirm that he was hoping in a just ruler who would overcome the curse and initiate a new creation (2 Sam. 23:3–7). Likewise, the writer of Hebrews stressed, "These all died in faith, not having received the things promised, but having seen them and greeted them from afar" (Heb. 11:13). The Old Testament remnant enjoyed some light; they themselves wrote of the Christ and hoped in him.

On the other hand, Jesus also declared that "many prophets and kings desired to see what you see, and did not see it" (Luke 10:24). It seems that we should understand Yahweh's prophets of old as truly seeing God's beauty and purposes and the hope that awaited them, while also affirming that they did not experience and, therefore, comprehend all that we do in Christ. For them, full disclosure awaited a later day.

First Peter 1:10–12 captures both sides of this interpretive framework. According to Peter, the prophets were themselves studiers of earlier revelation. And under the Spirit's guidance, they "searched and inquired carefully" to know *who* the Messiah would be and *when* he would appear. While they may not have known Jesus's name, they had a general sense of the type of person he would be and of when he would come, and they often learned this from studying the Scriptures (e.g., Ps. 119:2; Dan. 9:2). Revelation did indeed progress from the Old to New Testaments, but the development was often from conscious prediction to realized fulfillment, not simply prediction of which only God was originally aware but which we now recognize retrospectively.

The New Testament testifies that the Old Testament authors usually understood their end-time visions, truly hoped in the Messiah, and knew something of when he would come. Furthermore, interpreters should expect that the biblical authors' use of previous Scripture organically grows out of the earlier materials themselves, never contradicting them, because all Scripture comes from God (2 Tim. 3:16) and the prophets "searched and inquired carefully" (1 Pet. 1:10) and made Spirit-led interpretations (2 Pet. 1:20–21).

## The Rebels' Inability to Understand the Old Testament

The New Testament is also clear that the blindness associated with the old-covenant unbelieving majority continued into Christ's day. We see this incapacity, for example, in the religious leaders whom Jesus confronted numerous times (e.g., Matt. 12:3–7; Luke 16:31; John 5:39–40). The Jewish leaders were spiritually blind, unable to see how the Old Testament itself pointed to Christ.

The Gospels indicate the roots of such blindness. They speak of an innate wickedness that stands hostile to God, of hard hearts, of desires that are aligned with the devil, and of a passion for man's praise over God's glory (Matt. 16:3–4; 23:6; Mark 3:5; Luke 11:43; 20:46; John 8:42–44). The result was that these leaders could not hear God's voice or savor God's beauty and purposes in the Scriptures. And where the leaders went, the rest of the nation went also (John 12:37–41).

Likewise, other New Testament passages teach that the old-covenant age was one of ignorance and hardness (Acts 17:30; Eph. 4:18; 1 Pet. 1:14), with the devil keeping most of the world blind to God's glories culminating in Christ (2 Cor. 4:3–4). But in Jesus, new creation dawns, with gospel light breaking over the horizon and dispersing darkness and shadow (4:6).

Why would God extend such a season of hardness, ignorance, and blindness? If Romans 9:22–24 is any indication, Paul believes God purposed to move those receiving his mercy to marvel more at his manifold glory in Christ. The Lord made the darkness so deep and the night so long, that we upon whom the light has dawned may be able to savor even more the warmth, brilliance, and merciful glory of God bound up in his gift of Christ.

# The Remnant's Delayed Understanding of the Old Testament

The New Testament notes that some, such as Simeon, were anticipating Christ's coming and rightly grasped his person and work, including his mission of suffering (Luke 2:25–35). Nevertheless, many of the disciples closest to Jesus failed to recognize fully who he was and all that their Scriptures anticipated about him (see, e.g., Mark 4:13; 8:31–33).

Luke especially emphasized the disciples' lack of knowledge of the Old Testament. After his resurrection, Jesus challenged the two on the road to Emmaus for failing to "believe all that the prophets have spoken" (Luke 24:25). Nevertheless, he made them wise to the Old Testament's meaning (v. 27), thus fulfilling what Isaiah and Daniel said would come to pass (Isa. 29:18; Dan. 12:10). Likewise, Christ later appeared to his remaining followers and "opened their minds to understand the Scriptures" (Luke 24:45). The resurrected Christ now allows his followers to see things in the Bible that were there all along but imperceivable without the correct light and lens (see Rom. 16:25–26; 2 Cor. 3:14). In Christ, God "enlightens" the eyes of our hearts (Eph. 1:18).

John's Gospel in particular highlights how Christ's resurrection and glorification mark a turning point in the disciples' understanding of Scripture. In John 2:20–22, for example, Jesus's resurrection moved the disciples to embrace in a fresh way both "the Scripture and the word that Jesus had spoken." And as John 12:13–16 makes clear, only when the Father glorified his Son did Christ's followers connect how the Old Testament Scriptures testified to Christ's triumphal entry.

## Summary on the New Testament Perspective

The New Testament authors affirm that the Old Testament was written for Christians and that the prophets knew they were writing for our benefit. The prophets also knew something about Christ and the time of his coming, but the full meaning of their texts at times transcended their understanding. Thus, Paul can say, "You can perceive my insights into the mystery of Christ, which was not made known to the sons of men in other generations *as* it has now be revealed to his holy apostles and prophets by the Spirit" (Eph. 3:4–5).

Fulfilling the prophecy of Isaiah (Isa. 6:10; 53:1), the innate wickedness and hard-heartedness of most of the Jewish populace rendered them spiritually disabled. In judgment, God hardened them, so that they were unable to understand his Word or see his purposes culminating in Jesus (Rom. 11:7–8). Only "through Christ" is their blindness removed (2 Cor. 3:14).

Even at Jesus's birth, some like Simeon properly understood that the Christ's triumph would only come through tribulation. However, full understanding of Scripture's testimony about Jesus's death, resurrection, and global mission came to most of his disciples only after his resurrection.

# Old Testament Reflections on Grasping the Old Testament's Message

Even as the New Testament authors recognize that the Old Testament is Christian Scripture, the Old Testament authors knew that full understanding of their words awaited the messianic age. The seers, sages, and songwriters who gave us the Old Testament testify that they were speaking and writing not merely for old-covenant saints but also for new-covenant believers—those who would enjoy a relationship with God in the days of the Messiah and the new creation after Israel's exile. I will demonstrate this through four examples: Moses, Isaiah, Jeremiah, and Daniel. At the conclusion, we'll consider some implications of this fact for Christians approaching the Old Testament today.

## Moses's Hope for the Day His Words Will Be Obeyed

Moses's three most frequently used words to characterize Israel were "stubborn" (Deut. 9:6, 13; 10:16; 31:27), "unbelieving" (1:32; 9:23), and "rebellious" (9:7, 24; 31:27). His immediate audience was wicked (9:4–6, 27), and he affirmed that "even today while I am yet alive with you, you have been rebellious against the LORD. How much more after my death!" (31:27). Thus, Yahweh promised that the people's defiance would result in his pouring out his curses upon them (31:16–18).

Deuteronomy 29 tells the ultimate reason why Moses's immediate audience would not heed his words: Israel was spiritually ignorant of God's ways, blind to his glories, and deaf to his word (vv. 2, 4). They had been rebellious from the day Moses first met them (9:24), and their stubbornness was still present and would continue (9:6; 31:27, 29). In Moses's day, Yahweh had not overcome the resistance of the majority's hearts, and in alignment with his sovereign purposes for salvation history, he created the old covenant to bear a "ministry of death" and "condemnation" so that through Christ a superior new covenant might bear a "ministry of righteousness" (2 Cor. 3:7, 9).

Yahweh determined that he would not overcome Israel's crookedness and twistedness (Deut. 32:5; Acts 2:40; Phil. 2:15) until the prophet like Moses would rise (Deut. 18:15; 30:8, 14;

cf. Matt. 17:5). In the age of restoration, Yahweh would change the remnant's hearts and enable their love (Deut. 30:6). In this end-times period, the age we now identify with the new covenant and the church (cf. Rom. 2:29; 2 Cor. 3:6), Moses's message would finally be heeded (Deut. 30:8). Moses believed that his instruction would serve those in the age of heart circumcision far more than the rebels of his day.

## Isaiah's Hope for the Day His Words Will Be Heard

Israel's threefold spiritual disability (heart, eyes, ears) continued in the days of Isaiah, whom Yahweh called to "make the heart of this people dull, and their ears heavy, and blind their eyes" (Isa. 6:10). This would be the prophet's judgment cry until his land was laid waste, his people were destroyed, and all that remained was a "stump" or "holy seed" (6:11–13). Yahweh purposed that Israel's history would be characterized by "deep sleep" and the inability to "read" the Word. It was as if the Scriptures were sealed for the bulk of Isaiah's contemporaries (29:9–11).

Nevertheless, God promised that one day there would be a broad acceptance of the prophet's message (52:6; 54:13). Yahweh's law would go forth in "the latter days," and its recipients would include many from the "nations/peoples" (2:2–3; 51:4–5). That is, God would one day disclose himself to many who never sought him (Isa. 65:1; Rom. 10:20), and kings from many nations would see "that which had not been told them" (Isa. 52:15; Rom. 15:21). Isaiah associates the proclamation of this end-times instruction with the royal Servant (Isa. 42:1, 4).

Jesus indicated that through his own teaching God was fulfilling these promises by drawing a multiethnic people to himself (John 6:44–45; cf. Isa. 52:13). Christ's sheep would include some not from the Jewish fold (John 10:16; 11:51–52), yet all his sheep would "believe," "hear," and follow (10:26–27). To these awakened and responsive believers, the Lord would supply "the secret of the kingdom of God, but for those outside everything [would be] in parables, so that 'they may indeed see but not perceive, and may indeed hear but not understand, lest they should turn and be forgiven'" (Mark 4:11–12; citing Isa. 6:9–10). Isaiah himself saw that his writings would benefit a future generation more than they would the spiritually disabled of his day (Isa. 29:18; 30:8).

## Jeremiah's Hope for the Day His Words Will Guide

As with Isaiah, Yahweh told Jeremiah that his writing was intended for a post-exilic, restored community of God (Jer. 30:2–3). While some of Jeremiah's contemporaries would repent (36:2–3), most would not, for they retained the same stubbornness that characterized previous generations (7:23–28). Moreover, Jeremiah noted that only in the latter days would full understanding of his writings come: "The fierce anger of the LORD will not turn back until he has executed and accomplished the intentions of his mind. *In the latter days you will understand this*" (30:24–31:1). The "you" in this passage is plural, referring to the members of the new-covenant community (cf. 30:31–34).

Jeremiah's "latter days" of "understanding" are connected to (a) Israel/Judah's restoration from exile and reconciliation with God (30:10–11, 17–22; 31:1–40), (b) God's punishment of enemy nations (30:11, 16), (c) the rise of a ruler from the people's midst (30:21), and (d) the incorporation of foreigners into the one people of God (30:8–9). Christ and his church are now fulfilling Jeremiah's new-covenant hopes (Luke 22:20; 2 Cor.

3:6; Heb. 8:13; 9:15), which include every covenant member enjoying new knowledge and forgiveness of sins (Jer. 31:34; cf. Heb. 10:12–18; 1 John 2:20–21). This new knowledge aligns with the earlier promise of "understanding" (Jer. 30:24) and recalls Isaiah's promise that, following the work of the Servant, "all your children shall be taught by the LORD" (Isa. 54:13). God has "taught" all who have come to Christ, so that every Christian "knows" God in a personal way (John 6:45; 1 John 3:20–21; cf. Matt. 11:27).

## Daniel's Hope for the Day His Words Will Be Understood

The book of Daniel is filled with symbolic dreams, visions, and declarations—"mysteries" (Dan. 2:18–19, 27–30, 47; 4:9) that God often fully reveals to Daniel, so that "he understood the word and had understanding of the vision" (10:1; cf. 10:11–14). Indeed, Daniel grasped something of both the person and time of the Messiah's ministry (9:24–25; cf. 1 Pet. 1:10–11). Nevertheless, there are elaborations on these latter-day prophecies such that Daniel asserts, "I heard, but I did not understand" (Dan. 12:8) and that the Lord tells his prophet to "shut up the words and seal the book, until the time of the end" (12:4). The "end" is God's appointed period in salvation history when he would fully disclose his purposes to the wise (12:10).

Daniel envisioned that only at "the time of the end" would some people grasp the full meaning of his revelations. That is, the hiddenness of the Old Testament's meaning would be temporary for the remnant but permanent for the rebels. From a New Testament perspective, the first coming of Christ has inaugurated the promised days of realization, when the wise can both hear and understand God's words in this book. We see this in Matthew's Gospel, where, after speaking of "the

abomination of desolation spoken of by the prophet Daniel"
(Matt. 24:15; cf. 11:31; 12:11), an intrusive comment appears:
"*Let the reader understand*" (24:15). Matthew believes his read-
ers can grasp the mysteries of Daniel.

## Summary of the Old Testament Perspective

The texts above from Deuteronomy, Isaiah, Jeremiah, and
Daniel all suggest that Yahweh's prophets knew "that they
were serving not themselves" but us (1 Pet. 1:12), believers
upon whom the end of the ages has come (1 Cor. 10:11). The
various passages indicate that God withheld the full meaning
of his messages in at least two ways.

*First*, the prophets were convinced that the unbelieving
majority could not (due to God's punishment) and would not
(due to their sinfulness) heed any of their words. Nevertheless,
they also envisioned a day when Yahweh would overcome
spiritual disability, thus enabling a life-changing encounter
with him. At the rise of the child-king (Isa. 9:6–7), "the people
who walked in darkness" would see "a great light" (9:2; cf. Matt.
4:15–16). "In that day the deaf shall hear the words of a book,
and out of their gloom and darkness the eyes of the blind shall
see" (Isa. 29:18).

*Second*, Yahweh's prophets themselves did not always
fully grasp the meaning of their predictions and declarations.
Accordingly, Daniel could "understand" some visions (Dan.
10:1) while not "understanding" others (12:8). The faithful remnant would only fully comprehend God's intended meaning in
"the latter days" (Jer. 30:24), "the time of the end" (Dan. 12:4,
9–10). Thus, Jesus could say, "Many prophets and kings desired
to see what you see, and did not see it, and to hear what you hear,
and did not hear it" (Luke 10:24). A supernatural healing and
revelation would be required to create fresh responsiveness to

the Lord, thus awakening the heart to God's intended meaning of the Scriptures.

# Christ as Light and Lens for Reading the Old Testament Well

While the Old Testament prophets appear to have understood most of what they declared, God did not allow the majority of those in the old covenant to understand the prophets' words (e.g., Isa. 6:9–10). And as a judgment, the people's blindness continued into the days of Christ (Matt. 13:13–15). Nevertheless, fulfilling Old Testament predictions (e.g., Deut. 30:8), Jesus's teaching and work began disclosing truths to his disciples that the crowds did not understand: "To you has been given the secret [Greek *mystērion*] of the kingdom of God, but for those outside everything is in parables" (Mark 4:11–12).

The New Testament's "mystery" language appears to come from the book of Daniel, where the Greek translation uses the term *mystērion* ("mystery") to render the Aramaic *rāz* (2:18–19, 27–30, 47).[1] King Nebuchadnezzar has a troubling dream and then looks to Daniel for the full interpretive revelation. The "mystery" that God revealed to Daniel (v. 19) included both the initial dream and its interpretation, as the God in heaven "who reveals mysteries … made known to King Nebuchadnezzar what will be in the latter days" (v. 28). When Jesus alludes to this text by speaking about the "secret of the kingdom" (Mark 4:11–12), he indicates that the Old Testament's message would remain permanently hidden for some but temporarily hidden for others.

---

1. See G. K. Beale and Benjamin L. Gladd, *Hidden but Now Revealed: A Biblical Theology of Mystery* (Downers Grove, IL: InterVarsity Press, 2014), 29–46.

## Mystery in the New Testament

The New Testament employs the Greek word *mystērion* twenty-eight times, all as a technical term for an end-time reality largely hidden in the Old Testament but now disclosed more fully through Christ. All the New Testament occurrences deal with the end-times and are in some way linked to the Old Testament.

What was this "mystery"? In the Synoptic Gospels, the "mystery" relates to the unexpected, gradual, already-but-not-yet fulfillment of God's end-time reign (e.g., Mark 4:11). In Paul's epistles, which comprise twenty-one of the term's New Testament occurrences, the revealed "mystery" or "mysteries" refer to insight into God's end-times purposes (e.g., 1 Cor. 4:1) most directly associated with more fully understanding Christ and the gospel (e.g., Rom. 16:25). In Revelation, "mystery" relates to the nature of the church (Rev. 1:20) and the self-destructive nature of Babylon (17:5, 7).

## What Mystery Implies for Interpreting the Old Testament

Jesus, Paul, and John speak of God revealing a "mystery" to communicate how, in Christ, we gain full disclosure of things that God significantly hid from most in the old-covenant era. Strikingly, as Romans 16:25–27 teaches, the very "mystery" that is now revealed in and through Christ is also now made known to all nations *through* the Old Testament itself. In the coming of Christ, an era of understanding replaces an era of ignorance as light overcomes darkness and as God grants a fresh perspective on old truths (cf. Eph. 3:4–5).

Still, G. K. Beale and Benjamin Gladd rightly affirm that "full or 'complete' meaning is actually 'there' in the Old

Testament text; it is simply partially 'hidden' or latent, awaiting a later revelation, whereby the complete meaning of the text is revealed to the interpreter."[2] These parallel truths bear at least three implications for interpreting the Old Testament as the Christian Scripture it is: (a) Only those with spiritual sight can interpret the Old Testament correctly. (b) Jesus's life, death, and resurrection provide a necessary lens for fully understanding the Old Testament's meaning. (c) There is an organic relationship between the Old Testament's testimony and the meaning the New Testament authors attribute to it.

## A Relationship with Christ Is Necessary to Understand the Old Testament Rightly

Regarding many of his Jewish contemporaries, Paul declared, "For to this day, when they read the old covenant, that same veil remains unlifted, because only through Christ is it taken away" (2 Cor. 3:14). Those who understand "God's mystery, which is Christ" (Col. 2:2), are those to whom God has given "the light of the knowledge of the glory of God in the face of Jesus Christ" (2 Cor. 4:6). Indeed, Christ is "the radiance of the glory of God" (Heb. 1:3), and by his Spirit, he enlightens the eyes to see what the Old Testament revealed all along (Eph. 1:17–18).

To have the "mystery" of God's kingdom purposes revealed means, in part, that one's spiritual eyes have been opened to understand the Old Testament properly. Through rebirth, we become spiritual people who can spiritually discern and rightly understand spiritual truths (1 Cor. 2:13–14; cf. John 3:1–12). True Christians are the only ones who can rightly grasp all that God intends to communicate through the Old Testament.

---

2. Beale and Gladd, *Hidden but Now Revealed*, 330.

## Christ's Person and Work Clarify More Fully the Old Testament's Meaning

The Old Testament is filled with declarations, characters, events, and institutions that bear meaning in themselves but also find that meaning enhanced and clarified in Christ's person and work. For example, the meaning of events like the exodus or of objects like the sacrificial lamb are amplified when the New Testament treats Christ's saving work as an "exodus" (Luke 9:31) and calls him "the Lamb of God, who takes away the sin of the world" (John 1:29). Jesus's triumph validated him as the ultimate object of all Old Testament hopes, and this, in turn, transformed the apostles' reading of the Old Testament (2:22; 12:16).

Once Paul met the resurrected Christ, he, too, never read the Old Testament the same way. Indeed, as an Old Testament preacher, he "decided to know nothing ... except Jesus Christ and him crucified" (1 Cor. 2:2). At no stage in interpreting the Old Testament should Christians act as if Jesus has not come. Reading from the beginning through Scripture gets us to Christ, but once we find him, we must interpret all the Old Testament through him.

## The Way God Discloses the Mystery of Christ Signals Organic Connections between the Old and New

Passages such as Roman 16:25–26, 1 Peter 1:10–11, and 2 Peter 1:20–21 imply that the New Testament's use of the Old Testament is natural and unforced, aligning with the Old Testament's own innate meaning, contours, structures, language, and flow. The New Testament authors are making organic connections with the whole of Scripture on its own terms, in alignment with God's original intentions.

Other passages, such as Colossians 2:16–17, testify that the prophets often envisioned the very form we now enjoy, not only seeing the "shadow" but also embracing the "substance" that is Christ, though perhaps more like an acorn or sapling anticipates a great oak. Even if the Old Testament authors were not fully aware of all God was speaking through them, they would have affirmed retrospectively the trajectories that later biblical authors identify.

## Christ as Light and Lens

Scripture calls us to see both an organic unity and a progressive development between the Old and New Testaments. There is a natural connection between what the Old Testament human authors intended and what the New Testament human authors saw fulfilled in Jesus, but the Old Testament meaning is now often fuller, expanded, or deepened because through Christ God reveals the mystery. Jesus's saving work supplies the spiritual *light* that enables one's spiritual senses to see and savor rightly, and his person and work provide the interpretive *lens* for properly understanding and applying the Old Testament itself in a way that most completely magnifies God in Christ. Figure 1.1 unpacks what is happening with respect to Scripture's progressive revealing of Old Testament meaning, and figure 1.2 elucidates further the way Christ operates as a lens, supplying us a developed understanding of the Old Testament's meaning.

Revelation

No lens
(Mystery)

(Revelation)
Light

Light but no lens

Mystery

No lens, no light

Cross

Lens and light

No light
(Mystery)

Lens but no light

Lens
(Revelation)

Revelation

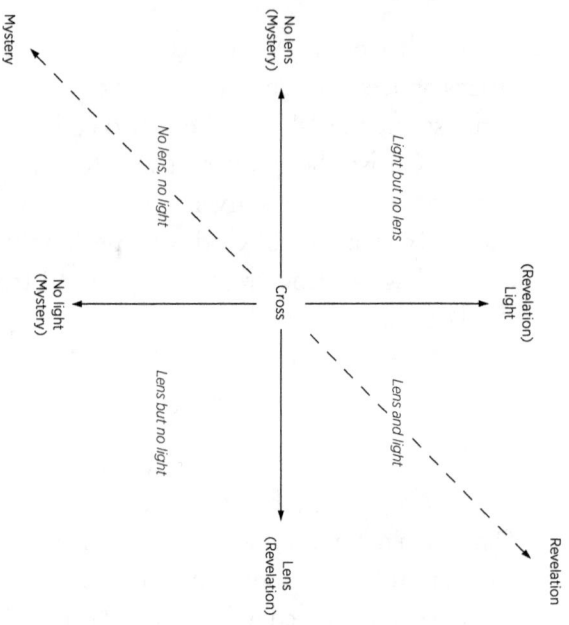

Old Testament Era ———— The Object—God's Self-Disclosure ————▶ New Testament Era

The left quadrants represent the era prior to the revelation of God's redemptive-historical purposes in Christ through the cross.

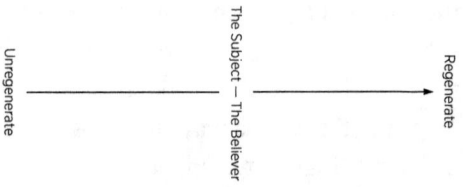

The horizontal x-axis represents progressive revelation.

The right quadrants represent the era consequent to the revelation of God's redemptive-historical purposes in Christ through the cross.

Unregenerate ———————— The Subject — The Believer ————————▶ Regenerate

The vertical y-axis represents regeneration

The upper quadrants represent sufficient (though not 100%) light in the soul (regenerate, believing).

The lower quadrants represent insufficient **light** in the soul (unregenerate, unbelieving).

Old Testament Anticipations    Christ    New Testament Realizations
(Partial Understanding)                            (Fuller Understanding)

Visions and declarations ————

Direct promises
and predictions ————                          Interpretation and meaning
                                              Fulfillment
Types/shadows ————                            Antitype/substance
(persons, events, things)                     Law of Christ

Law of Moses ————

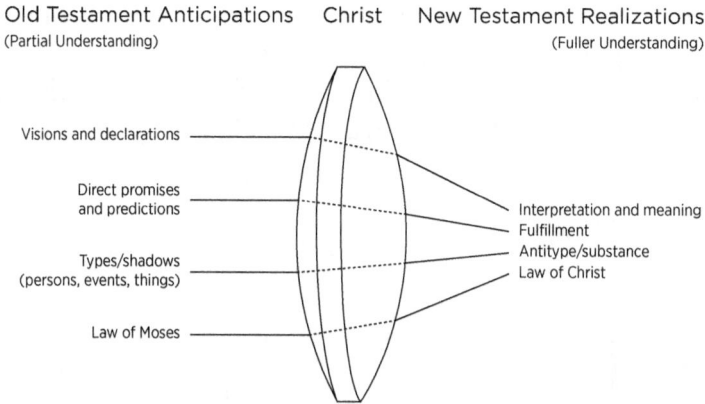

Figure 1.2. Interpreting the Old Testament through the Lens of Christ

# Conclusion

Both the Old and New Testament authors affirm that Jesus's only Bible—the Old Testament—is Christian Scripture. God intends that we interpret it as such and not as if Christ has not come. We must read the Scripture forward, backward, and forward again. The Old Testament prophets knew they were writing for new-covenant saints living in the days of the Christ. Bound up in the gospel of Jesus Christ is the revelation of a "mystery that was kept secret for long ages but … through the prophetic writings has been made known to all nations" (Rom. 16:25–26).

A relationship with Jesus is essential for rightly interpreting the Old Testament, for through him God enables understanding. By turning to Christ, "the veil is removed" (2 Cor. 3:16). The *light* of Christ supplies us the needed spiritual sight for understanding the things of God, and the *lens* of Christ's life, death, and resurrection provides the needed perspective for fully grasping the Old Testament's meaning. God wrote the

Old Testament for Christians, and he enables believing interpreters to grasp more fully than others both the meaning and
the intended effect of the initial three-fourths of the Christian
Scriptures. Jesus's Bible still matters for Christians.

# Two

# Seeing Well

## How Does Jesus's Bible Testify about Him?

*And beginning with Moses and all the Prophets, [Jesus]*
*interpreted for them in all the Scriptures the things*
*concerning himself. (Luke 24:27)*

Having embraced Jesus as the necessary light and lens, we are able to begin interpreting the Old Testament for what it is—Christian Scripture. Jesus is the one *through whom* and *for whom* we read the Old Testament. This chapter considers how Jesus's Bible truly "bears witness" about him (John 5:39). He said in every part of the Old Testament there were things "concerning himself" (Luke 24:27), and he highlighted that "to understand the Scriptures" means one sees a portrait of the Messiah's tribulation and triumph and the global saving mission he would generate (24:45–47). Is that what you see when you read the Old Testament?

Rightly seeing and celebrating Christ in the Old Testament requires a multi-form approach that accounts for Jesus's place within all of God's purposes in salvation history. This chapter overviews the biblical storyline, highlighting how it climaxes in Christ. It then supplies five principles for interpreting the Old Testament, notes three overlapping contexts that should guide all biblical interpretation, and then adds six more potential ways to magnify Jesus faithfully from his own Scriptures.

The chapter closes surveying Genesis to show how one Old Testament book bears foundational witness to Christ.

# KINGDOM: The Story of God's Glory in Christ

## God's Kingdom Program

The kingdom that Christ proclaimed and fulfilled (Luke 4:43; Acts 1:3) relates to God's reign over God's people in God's land for God's glory. God reigns, saves, and satisfies through covenant for his glory in Christ. This theme stands at the core of God's purposes from Genesis to Revelation.

When the Old and New Testaments are read together, at least seven stages are apparent in God's kingdom program (see fig. 2.1). The initial five are the foundation that is ultimately fulfilled in the last two. The acronym KINGDOM allows for easy memorization.

| Old Testament Narrative Foundation | K | 1. Kickoff and rebellion | Creation, fall, and flood |
| --- | --- | --- | --- |
| | I | 2. Instrument of blessing | Patriarchs |
| | N | 3. Nation saved and sent | Exodus, Sinai, and wilderness |
| | G | 4. Government in the land | Conquest and kingdoms |
| | D | 5. Dispersion and return | Exile and initial restoration |
| New Testament Narrative Fulfillment | O | 6. Overlap of the ages | Christ's work and the church age |
| | M | 7. Mission accomplished | Christ's return and kingdom consummation |

Figure 2.1. God's KINGDOM Plan

This story is marked by five overlapping covenants (Adamic/Noahic, Abrahamic, Mosaic, Davidic, and new), the progression of which detail God's purposes for humanity climaxing in Christ. The interrelationship of the covenants is like an hourglass, with the most universal scope occurring at the two ends and the work of Christ at the center (fig. 2.2). The titles of the initial four covenants relate to their covenant mediator, whereas the title "*new* covenant" signals how it supersedes the *old* Mosaic administration (Jer. 31:31–34; Heb. 8:6–13).

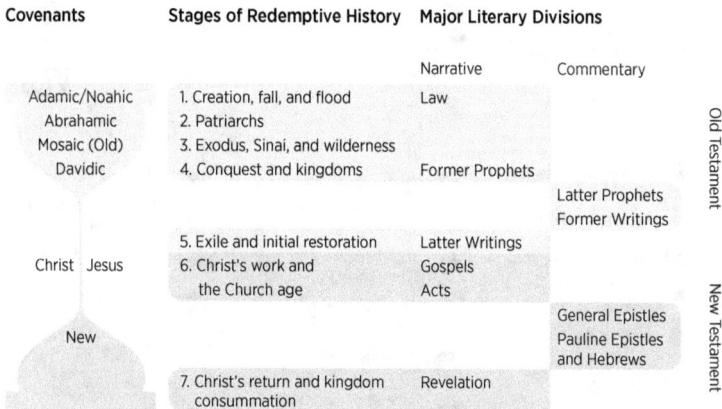

| Covenants | Stages of Redemptive History | Major Literary Divisions | | |
|---|---|---|---|---|
| | | Narrative | Commentary | |
| Adamic/Noahic | 1. Creation, fall, and flood | Law | | Old Testament |
| Abrahamic | 2. Patriarchs | | | |
| Mosaic (Old) | 3. Exodus, Sinai, and wilderness | | | |
| Davidic | 4. Conquest and kingdoms | Former Prophets | | |
| | | | Latter Prophets | |
| | | | Former Writings | |
| | 5. Exile and initial restoration | Latter Writings | | |
| Christ   Jesus | 6. Christ's work and | Gospels | | |
| | the Church age | Acts | | |
| | | | General Epistles | New Testament |
| New | | | Pauline Epistles | |
| | | | and Hebrews | |
| | 7. Christ's return and kingdom | Revelation | | |
| | consummation | | | |

Figure 2.2. Salvation History within the Flow of the Bible

Scripture's storyline indicates that Yahweh's definitive goal is to display himself as the supreme Savior, Sovereign, and Satisfier of the world, ultimately through his messianic representative. As such, the Bible tells *the story of God's glory in Christ*. Alongside the KINGDOM acronym, a set of images will help clarify the flow of God's purposes (fig. 2.3).

Figure 2.3. God's KINGDOM Plan through Images

## 1. Kickoff and Rebellion

God created humans to image him and commissioned them to "fill the earth and subdue it" (Gen. 1:28). But they failed to honor him and submitted to the authority of Satan (3:1–6), who in turn became the ruler of this world (cf. 2 Cor. 4:4). Because Adam acted as a covenantal head, God now counts the rest of humanity as having sinned in him (Rom. 5:12, 18–19). From fertilization, we are condemned sinners under God's just wrath (John 3:36; Eph. 2:1–3), and the result is that all rebel and fall short of glorifying God (Rom. 1:21–23; 3:23).

Before subjecting the world to futility (Gen. 3:16–19; Rom. 8:20–21), Yahweh promised to reestablish cosmic order through a human deliverer, who would decisively overcome the curse and the power of evil (Gen. 3:15). Sustained sin after the fall resulted in the flood (6:7–8), but God preserved a remnant and reaffirmed his covenant with creation (6:18; 8:21–9:1, 9–11). At the Tower of Babel, however, humans exalted themselves over God, resulting in Yahweh's punishment once again (11:1–9).

## 2. Instrument of Blessing

On the heels of Babel, Yahweh chose Abraham as the instrument through whom he would reverse the global curse. He commissioned him to "go" to Canaan and to "be a blessing" there (Gen. 12:1–3)—commands that indicate two phases in the Abrahamic covenant. First, in going to the land, Abraham would become a great nation (fulfilled in the Mosaic covenant). Second, through one of Abraham's representatives (i.e., the Messiah), God would restore a relationship of blessing with some from all the earth's families (fulfilled in the new covenant).

Though Sarah was barren (11:30), Abraham believed God's promise of offspring, and God counted that as righteousness (15:6). To exalt his faithfulness, Yahweh vowed to fulfill his land promise to Abraham's offspring (15:17–18). He also reaffirmed that he would bless the nations through a royal representative, now identified from Judah (22:17–18; 24:60; 49:8–10). Through this individual, Abraham would become a father of many nations (17:4–6), and the promised land (singular, 17:8) would expand to lands (plural, 22:17; 24:60; 26:3–4). For such ultimate good, God sent Joseph to Egypt to keep the Israelites alive amid famine, while awaiting the promised land (45:7–8; 50:20, 24–25).

## 3. Nation Saved and Sent

N ⚝ ⬗ 🝢 🝙 🝛

God fulfilled his promises by sustaining Israel through four hundred years of oppression (Exod. 1:7; cf. Gen. 15:13). For the sake of his reputation, he brought the plagues on Egypt and redeemed Israel from slavery (Exod. 7:5; 9:15–16). He gave Israel the Mosaic law to mediate his presence and display his holiness among the nations (19:5–6). He provided a means of atonement so that they could be near him (Lev. 9:3–6). And he restated his promise of a royal deliverer (Num. 24:7–9, 17–19).

Nevertheless, the majority were "rebellious" and "unbelieving" (Deut. 9:6–7, 23–24). Yahweh purposed not to overcome their hard-heartedness (29:4) but foretold how they would continue to rebel and suffer exile (4:25–29; 31:16–17). Nevertheless, out of his compassion (4:31), he would also restore them to the land (30:3–5), raise up a prophet like Moses (18:15–19), punish their enemies (30:7; 32:35), incorporate some from the nations (32:21, 43; 33:19), and cause all his people to love him and obey his voice (30:6, 8–14).

## 4. Government in the Land

G   👑  🌳  🏛  ♟

In Israel's conquest of the land, Yahweh kept his promises (Josh. 21:43–45) and exalted himself before the nations as the only true God (2:11). Nevertheless, without a faithful king, the people did what was right in their own eyes (Judg. 21:25), and God's word became rare (1 Sam. 3:1). They sought a king, which God granted, but they wanted him to replace Yahweh (8:7). Because they refused to heed the covenant and listen to the prophets, the united empire was divided (1 Kgs. 11:11, 13), and the northern and southern kingdoms came to a ruinous end—exile and a destroyed temple (2 Kgs. 17:6–23; 25:1–21).

Despite their rebellion, Yahweh graciously declared that he would fulfill his purposes through King David (2 Sam. 7:12, 16). One of David's offspring would be God's royal "Son," who would bless the nations and destroy God's enemies (Pss. 2:7–9; 72:17; cf. 2 Sam. 7:14). This Servant-King would also "bring back the preserved of Israel" and be "a light to the nations," extending Yahweh's reign to the ends of the earth (Isa. 49:3, 6). While guiltless (50:9; 53:9), he would satisfy God's wrath against sinners through a substitutionary death and, by his righteousness, "make many to be accounted righteous" (53:5, 10–11).

## 5. Dispersion and Return

D   🚫  🏛  ♟

Yahweh cast Israel from the land because the people failed to heed his voice (2 Kgs. 17:7; 2 Chr. 36:16). But from the depths of exile, Daniel pled for forgiveness and restoration (Dan. 9:18–19). Out of his boundless kindness (Lam. 3:22–23), God promised that he would establish "a kingdom that shall never be destroyed," that "one like a son of man" would receive "dominion and glory," and that all peoples "should serve him" (Dan. 2:44; 7:13–14).

In the end, Yahweh prevented the Jews from being annihilated (Esther) and restored them to the land (Ezra-Nehemiah). He commanded them to rebuild the temple (Hag. 1:8) and to honor him as the "great King" (Mal. 1:6, 14). Yet the story of God's glory still awaited its consummation. The royal Servant had yet to arrive, and Yahweh had not yet fully realized his kingdom purposes.

## 6. Overlap of the Ages

O ✝ 👑 🌍 ✨

Moving into the New Testament era, one of the mysteries of God's program was that Jesus would first come as suffering Servant and only in his second coming as conquering King (Heb. 9:28). He proclaimed "the year of the LORD's favor," but only later would he bring "the day of vengeance" (Isa. 61:2; Luke 4:19). Today we live in an overlap of the ages: Christ has delivered us from "the present evil age" (Gal. 1:4), yet only in a way that lets us taste "the powers of the age to come" (Heb. 6:5). Figure 2.4 visualizes the aspects of the kingdom that are *already* fully initiated but *not yet* finally consummated.

In the fullness of time, "God sent forth his Son" (Gal. 4:4) as the very Word that was God in the flesh (John 1:1, 14). He is the Christ, the promised royal Deliver, "the Lamb of God, who takes away the sins of the world" (1:29). By his life, death, and resurrection, he inaugurated the new covenant (Luke 22:20; Heb. 9:15) and new creation (2 Cor. 5:17). In the "great exchange" of the ages, God counts every believer's sin to Christ

First coming of Christ    Second coming of Christ

Old Age,    Church Age,    New Age,
Covenant,    Last Days    Covenant,
and Creation    "Already"    and Creation
    Gospel proclamation through
    suffering and sharing    "Not yet"

Sin and death    Righteousness and life

Figure 2.4. The Overlap of the Ages

and Christ's righteousness to every believer (Isa. 53:11; 2 Cor. 5:21).

Jesus and his apostles proclaimed the gospel of God's kingdom (Luke 4:43; Acts 1:3; 28:23), the good news "that Christ died for our sins in accordance with the Scriptures, that he was buried, that he was raised on the third day in accordance with the Scriptures, and that he appeared to Cephas, then to the twelve" (1 Cor. 15:3–5). By means of Spirit-empowered disciples bearing witness to Christ, God's reign has spread from Jerusalem to the ends of the earth (Acts 1:8). Under Christ's authority, the church must continue to make disciples of all nations for the sake of his name (Matt. 28:18–20; Rom. 1:5).

## 7. Mission Accomplished

The reigning King's return will be glorious (Matt. 16:27; 25:31), for we will see him "coming on the clouds of heaven with power and great glory" (24:30). Only those who "fear God and give him glory" will escape divine wrath when the Son of Man returns to be glorified (2 Thess. 1:9–10; Rev. 14:7).

Even now, those around the throne of the conquering Lion-Lamb are declaring him worthy to carry out God's purposes (Rev. 5:9–10). And the redeemed multitude will one day cry together, "Salvation belongs to our God … and to the Lamb!" (7:10). In that day, God's glory—localized in none other than the Lamb—will give his city light (21:23). His servants "will need no light or lamp or sun, for the Lord God will be their light, and they will reign forever and ever" (22:5), thus fulfilling their original calling to represent God on earth (Gen. 1:26–28).

In view of these realities, Jesus proclaims, "I am the root and the descendant of David, the bright morning star…. Surely I am coming soon" (Rev. 22:16, 20). And we say with John, "Amen. Come, Lord Jesus!" (22:20).

## Summary of God's KINGDOM Plan

From creation to consummation, God is guiding a kingdom program that culminates in Jesus. Both the Old and New Testaments are framed by *his*-story—a story of God's glory in Christ. In the Old Testament, God identifies the key players and problems and makes kingdom promises; in the New Testament, he supplies the solution and fulfills the promises, ultimately through King Jesus. All salvation history points to Christ, and through him God fulfills all earlier hopes, to the praise of his glorious grace (Eph. 1:6, 12).

# Treasuring Christ in All of Scripture

"And beginning with Moses and all the Prophets, he interpreted to them in all the Scriptures the things concerning himself" (Luke 24:27). The only Bible Jesus had was what we call the Old Testament, and he believed that his Scriptures bore witness about him (John 5:39) and that everything they said about him would be fulfilled (Luke 24:44).

Christ's followers, then, should be intent to magnify Jesus properly where he is evident. As the Puritan theologian John Owen wrote in 1684, "The revelation ... of Christ ... deserves the severest of our thoughts, the best of our meditations and our utmost diligence in them."[3] To accomplish this faithfully, one must employ a multifaceted approach that accounts for the centrality of Jesus in all God is doing in history.

## How to Engage in Christ-Centered Old Testament Interpretation

Considering the relationship of the Testaments and Scripture's unity centered on the divine Son, G. K. Beale has noted five principles that are rooted in the Old Testament's own story of salvation history and that guided the New Testament authors' interpretive conclusions:[4]

1. The New Testament authors always assume *corporate solidarity*, in which one can represent the many (e.g., Rom. 5:18–19).

2. Christ *represents the true (remnant) Israel* of the old covenant *and the true (consummate) Israel, the church*, of the new covenant (e.g., Isa. 49:3, 6; Luke 2:32).

3. God's wise and sovereign plan *unites salvation history* in such a way that earlier parts correspond to later parts (Isa. 46:9–10; Luke 16:16).

4. Christ has initiated (though not consummated) *the age of end-times fulfillment* (e.g., Heb. 1:2; 9:26).

5. Christ and his glory stand as the end-time center and goal of history, such that his life, death, and resurrection

---

3. John Owen, "Meditations on the Glory of Christ," in *The Works of John Owen*, ed. William H. Goold (Edinburgh: T&T Clark, 1862), 1:275.
4. G. K. Beale, "Did Jesus and His Followers Preach the Right Doctrine from the Wrong Texts?," *Themelios* 14 (1989): 90. The present author has added the scriptural references.

provide *the key to interpreting the Old Testament and
its promises.*

These principles directed the way Jesus and the apostles interpreted Scripture, and they should inform every Christian
approach to the Old Testament.

Furthermore, the fact that God authored Scripture and
gives it an overarching unity demands that all Old Testament
interpretation consider three distinct but overlapping contexts:[5]

1. The *close context* focuses on a passage's immediate literary setting within the whole book. Here we observe
   carefully what and how the text communicates,
   accounting for both the words and the theology that
   shapes those words.

2. The *continuing context* considers the passage within God's story of salvation. We examine how a text is
   informed by previous Scripture and contributes to
   God's unfolding kingdom drama.

3. The *complete context* concerns a text's placement and
   use within the broader canon. We consider how later
   Scripture might use the passage, remembering that the
   divine authorship of Scripture allows later passages to
   clarify, enhance, or deepen the meaning of earlier texts.

Only by considering all three contexts will Christian inter-
preters be able to fully grasp God's intended meaning of Old
Testament passages and understand how those texts point to
Christ.

---

5. These categories are drawn from Trent Hunter and Stephen J. Wellum, *Christ from Beginning to End:
How the Full Story of Scripture Reveals the Full Glory of Christ* (Grand Rapids: Zondervan, 2018), 42–69.

## Six More Ways to See and Celebrate Christ in the Old Testament

Along with tracing Scripture's kingdom program climaxing in Jesus (see above), the salvation-historical, Christocentric model presented here proposes at least six other ways God exalts Jesus in the Old Testament.

### See and Celebrate Christ through the Old Testament's Direct Messianic Predictions

In Acts 3:18, 24, Peter stresses that every one of the prophets, from Moses onward, anticipated the Messiah's suffering and the days of the church. The Old Testament, then, is loaded with explicit and implicit direct messianic predictions. For example, Moses records that Yahweh promised Abraham that a single male offspring would "possess the gate of his enemies" and that "all the nations of the earth" would regard themselves "blessed" in him (Gen. 22:17b–18). Paul, then, notes how in Christ God fulfilled his promise to bless the Gentiles (Gal. 3:8, 14). So, when you read the Old Testament's messianic predictions, see and savor how the divine Son realizes these hopes.

### See and Celebrate Christ through Similarities and Contrasts of the Old and New Ages, Creations, and Covenants

Jesus's saving work creates both continuities and discontinuities between the old and new ages, creations, and covenants. For instance, while both covenants contain a similar structure (i.e., God first redeems and then calls his people to obey), only the new covenant supplies freedom from sin and power for obedience to *all* covenant members (Jer. 31:33–34). Similarly, whereas God used the blood of bulls and goats to atone in the old covenant, Christ's substitutionary sacrifice alone provides the ground for eternal redemption (Heb. 9:11–14). These kinds of similarities and contrasts encourage a messianic reading of the Old Testament. We can treasure Christ's work by identifying the patterns and transformations.

## See and Celebrate Christ through the Old Testament's Typology

God structured salvation history in such a way that certain Old Testament characters (e.g., Adam, Moses, David), events (e.g., the flood, exodus, return to the land), and institutions or objects (e.g., the Passover lamb, temple, priesthood) bear meanings that clarify, color, and predictively anticipate the Messiah's life and work. The New Testament refers to these pointers as "types" or "examples" (Rom. 5:14; 1 Cor. 10:6). They find their counter in Jesus as their ultimate realization ("antitype"). When you identify Old Testament types that clarify and anticipate Christ's person and work, see and celebrate the Son as the substance of all earlier shadows.

## See and Celebrate Christ through Yahweh's Identity and Activity

Jesus said that no one has ever seen God the Father except the Son (John 6:46) and that "whoever has seen me has seen the Father" (14:9). Minimally, this means that those who saw God in the Old Testament (e.g., Exod. 24:11) were enjoying but partial glimpses of Jesus's glory (33:18–23; cf. 2 Cor. 4:6). It may also imply that, at least in some instances where Yahweh becomes embodied in human form (e.g., Gen. 18:22), we are meeting the preincarnate Son. In brief, when we meet Yahweh in the Old Testament, we are catching glimpses of the coming Christ. As such, when you revel in Yahweh's identity and activity, treasure the divine Son.

## See and Celebrate Christ through the Ethical Ideals of Old Testament Law and Wisdom

The laws and wise sayings in the Old Testament are sources for magnifying the greatness of Christ on our behalf. He is the perfect embodiment of God's character and the ideal image of law keeping and wisdom. Paul stressed both that in the law we have "the embodiment of knowledge and truth" (Rom. 2:20) and that "the law is holy, and the commandment is holy and righteous and good" (7:12). The same can be said of Christ, who remained sinless (Heb. 4:15) and "became to us wisdom from God" (1 Cor. 1:30). Therefore, when you observe how the Old Testament law and wisdom express ethical ideals, celebrate the justifying work of the divine Son (Rom. 5:18–19).

## See and Celebrate Christ by Using the Old Testament to Instruct Others

Jesus's coming unlocks the significance of the Old Testament (2 Cor. 3:14; 2 Tim. 3:15), and through him we now have access to a massive amount of Scripture that can clarify how to love God and neighbor (Rom. 16:25–26). Moreover, God now empowers us in Christ to keep the "precepts" of the law, as we live with circumcised hearts by the power of the Spirit (Rom. 2:26, 29). Christ is our teacher, and his own fulfillment of the law now clarifies for us what it means to follow God (Matt. 5:17–19). When we use the Old Testament to instruct or guide others, calling them to love and thus fulfill the law (Rom. 13:8–10; cf. 2 Tim. 3:16), we should delight in the sanctifying work of the divine Son.

## Synthesis of the Seven Ways to See and Celebrate Christ

This chapter has supplied seven ways to treasure Christ in the Old Testament. Not all operate at the same time, but each of these provides readers and teachers of Scripture fresh avenues to make much of Jesus.

1. Consider the Old Testament's salvation-historical trajectories
2. See the Old Testament's direct messianic predictions
3. Recognize similarities and contrasts within salvation history
4. Identify Old Testament types
5. Revel in Yahweh's identity and activity
6. Observe the Old Testament's ethical ideals
7. Use the Old Testament to instruct others

Figure 2.5. Seven Ways to See and Celebrate Christ in
the Old Testament

May we increasingly learn to proclaim "Jesus Christ and him crucified" (1 Cor. 2:2) from the initial three-fourths of the Christian Scriptures. To consider how this could be done, let's consider the Bible's first book as a case study in seeing and celebrating Christ in the Old Testament.

# Jesus in Genesis: A Case Study

While Exodus–Deuteronomy details Israel's calling as a holy nation (Exod. 19:5–6), Genesis clarifies the global context of that calling and the hope of a royal Deliverer. Accordingly, it describes the initial two KINGDOM stages: Kickoff and Rebellion (creation, fall, flood) and Instrument of Blessing (the patriarchs). It also details the initial two biblical covenants: the Adamic/Noahic and the Abrahamic covenants.

## Thought Flow

Genesis opens with a preface in 1:1–2:3 (part 1). It then comprises ten units headed by the phrase "the generations of," which are grouped into five larger units, given the fronting of the Hebrew word for "and" (see fig. 2.6).

| Part | Section | The Preface and "Generations" Units | Genre |
|---|---|---|---|
| 1 | | Preface: Biblical worldview foundations (1:1–2:3) | |
| 2 | i | These are the generations of the heavens and the earth (2:4–4:26) | N (+LG/SG) |
| 3A | ii | This is the book of the generations of Adam (5:1–6:8) | LG (+N) |
| | iii | These are the generations of Noah (6:9–9:29) | N |
| | | And these are the generations of Noah's Sons (10:1–11:9) | SG (+N) |
| 3B | iv | These are the generations of Shem (11:10–26) | LG |
| | | And these are the generations of Terah (11:27–25:11) | N (+SG) |
| | | And these are the generations of Ishmael (25:12–18) | SG |
| | | And these are the generations of Isaac (25:19–35:29) | N |
| | | And these are the generations of Esau (36:1–8, 9–37:1) | SG (+N+SG) |
| | v | These are the generations of Jacob (37:2–50:26) | N (+SG+N) |
| KEY: N = Narrative; LG = Linear Genealogy; SG = Segmented Genealogy | | | |

Figure 2.6. Genesis's Structure

The first of these "generations" units (part 2) has the only heading that does not include a human name (2:4); both this and the context suggest that the ensuing section (2:4–4:26) introduces the redemptive story that follows. As figure 2.7 shows, this section also clarifies the world's *need for blessing*, as it details humanity's covenantal purpose (2:4–25); humanity's sin, God's curse, and its aftermath (3:1–4:26); and Yahweh's promise of a curse-overcoming offspring (3:15).

After this, two linear genealogies (5:1–6:8; 11:10–26) introduce two parallel units that develop the world's *hope for blessing* (5:1–11:9; 11:10–50:26). Part 3A reports the kingdom hope from Adam to Noah (5:1–6:8) and then describes how Yahweh protected the promised line and renewed his covenant with creation in the wake of the flood (6:9–11:9). Part 3B documents the perpetuation of kingdom hope from Shem to Terah and clarifies how God will use Abraham and his offspring to bless the nations (11:10–37:1). It then closes with a recounting of the promised line's preservation in Egypt, while also developing the hope for a royal Deliverer (37:2–50:26).

## Major Movements

### Preface (Gen. 1:1–2:3)

At creation's climax, God shapes humans in his image (1:26–27) and charges them to "be fruitful and multiply and fill the earth and subdue it and have dominion" (1:28). From the start, God's covenant with creation stresses the themes of progeny, property, and power, all themes that resurface in Scripture's covenantal progression culminating in Christ. The narrator characterizes the commission as a blessing, meaning that humankind would only increase and rule as God's representatives if he empowered them to do so.

I. **God's Blessing-Commission: Preface (1:1–2:3):** God purposes that humanity rule his world as his image bearers

II. **The Need for Blessing (2:4–4:26):** Humanity rebels and God curses the world yet promises a curse overcoming offspring

III. **The Hope for Blessing (5:1–50:26):** God preserves humanity and provides a way for the world to enjoy kingdom blessing

    A. God reaffirms humanity's blessing-commission (5:1–11:9)

        1. God perpetuates kingdom hope from Adam to Noah in the context of threat (5:1–6:8)

        2. God protects the promised line and restores humanity's kingdom purpose in the context of punishment (6:9–11:9)

    B. God declares how his kingdom blessing will reach the world (11:10–50:26)

        1. God perpetuates kingdom hope from Shem to Terah and elevates Abraham and his offspring as the agents for bringing kingdom blessing to the world (11:10–37:1)

        2. God preserves the promised line through famine in Egypt and develops kingdom hope for a royal deliverer from Judah (37:2–50:26)

Figure 2.7. Genesis's Thought Flow

**See and Celebrate Christ in the Old Testament**
***Way 5: Revel in Yahweh's Identity and Activity***
God's role as Creator (Gen. 1:1) allows us to see and celebrate Christ, who was "in the beginning with God" and without whom "was not anything made that was made" (John 1:2–3; cf. Col. 1:16).

## The Generations of the Heavens and the Earth (Gen. 2:4–4:26)

Yahweh set the first man as head over his creation (2:15–17) and then provided him a wife from his own body (2:21–25). When Adam rebelled (3:1–6), he secured his own death and the death of those he represented (2:17; Rom. 5:12). He also transferred the world's rule to the evil serpent (1 John 5:19).

A new "Adam" figure, operating as a new-covenantal head, would be the only one to reverse such a curse (Rom. 5:18–19).

God subjected creation to "futility," but he did so "in hope" (8:20), for when he cursed the serpent, he promised: "I will put enmity between you and the woman, and between your offspring and her offspring; he shall bruise your head, and you shall bruise his heel" (Gen. 3:15). The singular pronoun "he"

---

**See and Celebrate Christ in the Old Testament**
*Way 4: Identify Old Testament Types*
Paul notes that Adam "was a type of the one who was to come....
For as by the one man's disobedience the many were made sinners,
so by the one man's obedience the many will be made righteous"
(Rom. 5:14, 19).

---

here indicates the "offspring" is a male *individual*, who would triumph over the evil serpent, thus reversing the curse and bringing new creation.[6]

---

**See and Celebrate Christ in the Old Testament**
*Ways 2 and 4: See the Old Testament's Direct Messianic Predictions and Identify Old Testament Types*
Genesis 3:15 is direct messianic prophecy anticipating Christ, and
Revelation 12:1-6, 17 recalls the verse with respect to Jesus. Along
with being the "last Adam" (1 Cor. 15:45), Christ is the antitypical
human, who perfectly images God (2 Cor. 4:4; Col. 1:15).

---

## The Generations of Adam, Noah, and His Sons (Gen. 5:1–11:9)

The genealogy from Adam to Noah highlights how God was preserving the "living," whose hope was in the one to come. In typological foreshadowing of Genesis 3:15's fulfillment, Lamech declared that his son Noah would overcome the curse

---

6. C. John Collins, "A Syntactical Note (Genesis 3:15): Is the Woman's Seed Singular or Plural?," *Tyndale Bulletin* 48.1 (1997): 139–48.

(5:29). Through Noah, God preserved a remnant (8:14–19) and reaffirmed his blessing-commission and covenant with creation (9:1, 7, 9–17). By substitutionary atonement (8:20–22), which anticipated Christ's saving work, Yahweh purchased common grace for all (Matt. 5:45).

---

**See and Celebrate Christ in the Old Testament**
*Way 7: Use the Old Testament to Instruct Others*
That "Noah walked with God" and "was a righteous man, blameless in his generation" (Gen. 6:8–9) magnifies Christ as the one whose sanctifying power makes justified saints holy–even Old Testament saints, thus providing us an example by which to live (Heb. 11:7).

---

Following the flood, evil intentions led humans to rebel again (Gen. 11:1–6). So, Yahweh confused their languages and dispersed them throughout the earth (11:7–9). Specifically, those dispersed were the "clans/families" of Shem, Ham, and Japheth, which together became seventy "nations" (10:32; 11:7–9). Yahweh would incorporate a remnant of these "families" (12:3; 28:14) and "nations" (18:18; 22:18; 26:4) into his global saving purposes.

## The Generations of Shem, Terah, Ishmael, Isaac, Esau, and Jacob (Gen. 11:10–50:26)

*Shem's and Terah's Generations (Gen. 11:10–26; 11:27–25:11).* The heading "the generations of Shem" (11:10) recalls Shem's elevation among his brothers in Yahweh's kingdom program (9:26–27), and Shem's genealogy to Terah again highlights how Yahweh preserved people in every generation who hoped in the coming offspring (11:10–26). The progenitor in the next "generations" heading is Terah (11:27), because Moses wanted to devote much of the next section to the story of Abram, later named Abraham.

The plot develops significantly when Yahweh commissions Abram to "go" to Canaan and there "be a blessing." As figure 2.8 shows, these two coordinated commands (12:1b, 2d) are each followed by one or more conditional promises (12:2abc, 3ab), and the second command-promise unit includes the ultimate promissory result: global blessing (12:3c). The two units indicate how God would reverse the punishments of property and progeny promised in Genesis 3:14–19.[7]

---

**See and Celebrate Christ in the Old Testament**
*Ways 1 and 7: Consider the Old Testament's Salvation-Historical Trajectories and Use the Old Testament to Instruct Others*
Through the two commands—"go" and "be a blessing"—in Genesis 12:1-3, Yahweh sets a salvation-historical trajectory that moves through Abraham's becoming a father of one nation (the old covenant, Gen. 17:7-8) to Christ's saving work that makes Abraham the father of many nations (the new covenant, 17:4-6). Hearing the commands and believing that the promises were desirable and that the promise maker was trustworthy, "Abraham went" (Gen. 12:4) and by this provided a model of faith and obedience for every believer (Heb. 11:8). We can follow the patriarch's pattern only through Jesus, who is "the founder and perfecter of our faith" (Heb. 12:2).

---

The two units also foresee two major phases in God's saving drama. Phase one relates to Abraham fathering a nation centered in Canaan. Yahweh would fulfill this through the Mosaic covenant (15:13, 18; 17:8). Phase two would occur when Abraham's representative blessed the families Yahweh dispersed (12:2d–3). This would happen only when Abraham's offspring perfectly obeyed (18:18–19)—something realized only through Abraham's ultimate offspring who blesses the world (22:17–18; Gal. 3:14, 16, 29). Jesus does this through his perfect life, culminating in his death and resurrection (Phil. 2:8; 1 Pet. 2:22).

---

7. James M. Hamilton Jr., "The Seed of the Woman and the Blessing of Abraham," *Tyndale Bulletin* 58.2 (2007): 253–73.

| | And Yahweh said to Abram, | 1a |
|---|---|---|
| **Phase 1:** **Realized in the Mosaic Covenant** | "**Go** from your land and your kindred and your father's house to the land that I will show you, | b |
| | so that I may make you into a great nation, | 2a |
| | and may bless you, | b |
| | and may make your name great. | c |
| **Phase 2:** **Realized in the New Covenant** | **Then be** a blessing, | d |
| | so that I may bless those who bless you, | 3a |
| | but him who dishonors you I will curse, | b |
| | with the result that in you all the families of the ground may be blessed." | c |

Figure 2.8. The Structure of Genesis 12:1–3 (Author's Translation)

Through Isaac God would affirm his covenant and name the promised offspring (Gen. 17:19, 21; 21:12). This one would serve as Abraham's greater "son," through whom—by his substitutionary sacrifice—"the LORD will provide" pardon for many (22:13–14; cf. Rom. 8:32). By becoming numerous, this

> **See and Celebrate Christ in the Old Testament**
> **Way 6: Observe the Old Testament's Ethical Ideals**
> "Righteousness" was the ethical goal of law keeping (Deut. 6:25). Yet God credits righteousness to Abraham by faith apart from works (Gen. 15:16), thus justifying the ungodly (Rom. 4:5) based on Christ's perfect righteousness, which leads to "justification and life for all men" (5:18; cf. 3:21–26).

singular "offspring" will conquer his enemies' gate (Gen. 22:17; 24:60; cf. 26:3) and stand as the one in whom all nations count themselves blessed (22:18; cf. 26:4), thus expanding the patriarch's fatherhood (17:4). Upon Abraham's death, Yahweh blessed Isaac (25:11).

*Ishmael's, Isaac's, and Esau's Generations (Gen. 25:12–18; 25:19–35:29; 36:1–37:1).* At this point, the narrative includes a genealogy devoted to "the generations of Ishmael" (25:12–18), whom Hagar bore to Abraham and whom Yahweh said would become a great nation but not as the agent of his covenant (22:20–21). His descendants represent those living under a curse, in need of the blessing Abraham's offspring would supply.

With the narrative associated with "the generations of Isaac" (25:19–35:29), Yahweh reaffirmed and developed his patriarchal promises. Rebekah's twins would be rival nations/peoples, with the older serving the younger (25:23)—something soon realized when the elder Esau sold his birthright to Jacob (25:29–34). Furthermore, in commissioning Isaac to sojourn in the "land" (singular), God promised his presence and blessing, which would include the promised offspring inheriting "lands" (plural; 26:3–4). Quoting this exact promise, which is tied to the earlier promise in Genesis 22:17–18, Paul identified Christ as the "offspring" that blesses the world (Gal. 3:16, 29).

Lastly, we learn of Rachel and Isaac's deaths just before two genealogies associated with "the generations of Esau" (36:1–37:1). The content of these, again, details those surrounding Israel who needed Yahweh's blessing.

> **See and Celebrate Christ in the Old Testament**
> *Way 3: Recognize Similarities and Contrasts within Salvation History*
> The continuity and discontinuity between the "land" (singular in Gen. 12:1–2; 15:18; cf. Josh. 21:43; 1 Kgs. 4:21) and "lands" (plural in Gen. 26:3–4; "world" in Rom. 4:13) magnifies Christ as the one in whom this salvation-historical development happens, culminating in the new heavens and earth.

## Jacob's Generations (Gen. 37:2–50:26)

The book's final chapters are devoted to "the generations of Jacob" (37:2–50:26), recording the preservation of Jacob's twelve sons and their descendants, who would become the nation of Israel and through whom the promised Deliverer would rise. While Joseph is the eleventh born son, his father treats him as the firstborn (37:3–4), and the narrative anticipates his rise above his brothers (37:5–11). Yet his brothers sell him into slavery (37:28).

After a brief interlude on Judah's offspring (chap. 38), the narrative returns to Joseph, who moves from Egyptian prisoner

> **See and Celebrate Christ in the Old Testament**
> *Way 2: See the Old Testament's direct messianic predictions*
> Yahweh's promise that "the scepter shall not depart" from the "lion"-like Judah and that a king would rise to whom "shall be the obedience of the peoples" (Gen. 49:9–10) directly predicts the rise of Jesus Christ, who is "the son of David, the son of Abraham" (Matt. 1:1), and "the Lion of the tribe of Judah" (Rev. 5:5). He will reign on "the throne of his father David," and "of his kingdom there will be no end" (Luke 1:32–33).

to Egyptian viceroy (i.e., second-in-command) (39:1–41:40). Yahweh uses him to preserve life during a famine (45:5, 7). Once his family secured refuge in Egypt (47:26–27), Jacob declared

Yahweh's special blessing on Joseph's offspring (49:22–26). Concerning Judah, though, he also declared that kingship would remain in his line until the promised one comes (49:8–12). Joseph would retain the blessing of the firstborn, then, but Judah would be the one through whom the offspring-Deliverer would rise "in the last days" (49:1).

## Conclusion

This chapter has proposed seven different ways for making much of Christ in the Old Testament. See and celebrate him by:

- Considering the Old Testament's salvation-historical trajectories;
- Seeing the Old Testament's direct messianic predictions;
- Recognizing similarities and contrasts within salvation history;
- Identifying Old Testament types;
- Reveling in Yahweh's identity and activity;
- Observing the Old Testament's ethical ideals; and
- Using the Old Testament to instruct others.

Furthermore, reading a book like Genesis within its close, continuing, and complete contexts reveals that it details gospel hope climaxing in Christ. Its *main idea* is this: Despite humanity's losing the blessing of eternally reigning over a very good world as God's image bearers, Yahweh will restore this blessing to all nations when they place their faith in the woman's royal offspring, who will descend from Abraham, Isaac, Jacob, and Judah, crush the serpent, and claim all lands. In short, Genesis is Christian Scripture in which we can see and celebrate the Messiah and the gospel's hope. Observing and evaluating other Old

Testament books carefully should allow prayerful Christians to enjoy similar results.

# Three

# Hoping Well

## How Does Jesus Secure Every Divine Promise?

*For all the promises of God find their Yes in [Jesus.]*
*That is why it is through him that we utter our Amen*
*to God for his glory. (2 Cor. 1:20)*

What biblical promises are for Christians? Should believers today claim all Old Testament promises as their own since God gave those promises to a different people and under a different covenant? This chapter considers why and how *every* promise is "Yes" in Christ (2 Cor. 1:20). Through Jesus, God empowers Christians to appropriate Old Testament promises faithfully without abusing them. This chapter argues this thesis by considering the importance and challenge of claiming Old Testament promises, supplying five principles that guided the New Testament authors when appropriating Old Testament promises, and four different ways that Jesus's coming influences past promises.

## Should Christians Hope in Old Testament Promises?

To promise is to assure that one will do a particular thing or that a certain thing will happen. God's promises of blessing and curse play a key role in helping believers grow in sanctification (2 Pet. 1:4) and suffer with hope (Ps. 119:50). Promises are one of Scripture's unifying motifs, and some scholars have even argued that divine promise is *the* theological center of the Christian canon.[1]

## The Importance of God's Promises for Christians

God's promises confront a host of sins. For instance, if we are *anxious* about having enough food, clothing, and shelter, we heed Jesus's call to "seek first the kingdom of God," confident that "all these things will be added to [us]" (Matt. 6:33). When *covetousness* rises in our soul, we nurture contentment by recalling promises like, "I will never leave you nor forsake you" (Heb. 13:5). And in our passion for sexual purity, we fight *lust* by remembering the promise, "Blessed are the pure in heart, for they shall see God" (Matt. 5:8).

But not only this. When we face suffering, God's promises in Scripture supply one of our bulwarks of hope. As the psalmist declared, "This is my comfort in my affliction, that your promise gives me life" (Ps. 119:50). Christians must recognize the importance of God's promises — even Old Testament ones — for both our pursuit of holiness and our hope in suffering.

## God's Major Promises in Scripture

Addressing the first human, God's initial promise in Scripture is this: "In the day that you eat of [the forbidden tree] you shall surely die" (Gen. 2:17). Following their disobedience, Adam and Eve's spiritual death and exile from the garden proved Yahweh's faithfulness (3:22–24). But even prior to punishing

---

1. See, e.g., Walter C. Kaiser Jr., *The Promise-Plan of God: A Biblical Theology of the Old and New Testaments* (Grand Rapids: Zondervan, 2008).

them, Yahweh also cursed the serpent and promised that one of the woman's male descendants would triumph over him (3:15). From this point forward, salvation history discloses a hope in this coming offspring and in the global reconciliation that he would ignite.

Scripture next anticipates the curse's reversal in God's promises to the patriarchs, which relate to offspring, land, blessing, and divine presence.

1. *Offspring.* God will grow the patriarchs into a great nation (12:2; 46:3) and raise up kings in their midst who will influence the nations (17:6, 16; 49:10). In time, Abraham's fatherhood would include the nation of Israel *and* the nations more broadly (17:4–6, 16). This would occur through the rise of a single male royal descendant (22:18).

2. *Land.* Yahweh committed not only to give the patriarchs the land of Canaan (17:8); he also promised that a royal deliverer would expand it to include the rest of the world (22:17–18; 26:3–4)—realities that are now inaugurated in Christ's first coming and will be consummated in his second.

3. *Blessing.* God promised to bless Abraham and his offspring (12:2; 49:25–26). Ultimately, he would use one of Abraham's descendants to overcome his enemies (22:17; 24:60) and bless the nations (12:3; 22:18; 26:4).

4. *Presence.* From the beginning, God's blessing is associated with humanity's ability to represent him rightly in the world (1:28). By contrast, curse brings only tragedy. In such a setting, Yahweh affirmed that he would be present with the patriarchs and their offspring (9:27; 48:21).

Most of these patriarchal promises are initially and partially fulfilled in the Mosaic covenant, but all are only completely fulfilled through Christ and the new covenant.

## Some Reflections on Prosperity Preaching

If "all the promises of God find their 'Yes' in [Jesus]" (2 Cor. 1:20), should we as Christians claim all the Bible's promises as our own, including the Old Testament's? Prosperity preachers quickly answer, "Yes," contending that Christ has already secured every spiritual *and* physical blessing for us to enjoy *today*.

### Health and Wealth

Consider the words of prosperity author Gordon Lindsay:

> In Deuteronomy 28 God lists various diseases that will come upon the Israelites if they do not obey the voice of the LORD…. Some contend … that sickness was spoken of as a curse *then*, but since today we are under a different covenant, the situation concerning sickness and healing is reversed…. How ridiculous! The New Testament teaches divine health for the believer just as much as the Old Testament does.[2]

Similarly, Oral Roberts appeals to passages like 2 Corinthians 9:10 when offering the following financial principle: "If you sow it, God will grow it."[3]

Later in this chapter we will consider the relationship of old-covenant blessings and curses to Christians today, showing

2. Gordon Lindsay, *The Bible Secret of Divine Health* (Santa Ana, CA: Trinity Broadcasting Network, 1987), 19–20, 21–22.
3. Oral Roberts, *If You Need to Be Blessed Financially Do These Things* (Tulsa, OK: Oral Roberts Evangelistic Association, 1982), 5.

how prosperity theology fails to account rightly for the progression of the covenants. Now, we can affirm that the principle of sowing and reaping is biblical: "He who supplies seed to the sower and bread for food will supply and multiply your seed for sowing and increase the harvest of your righteousness" (2 Cor. 9:10). However, the way prosperity preachers apply this text and others fails to account for the broader biblical context. For example, the apostle Paul introduces his discussion of sowing and reaping with the words, "Though [Christ] was rich, yet for your sake he became poor, so that you by his poverty might become rich" (2 Cor. 8:9). Prosperity teachers assume that riches and poverty here mean material gain and lack, respectively. However, when Paul speaks of Jesus's shift from rich to poor, he refers not to a change in Christ's economic status but to his incarnation and his willingness to die on our behalf (cf. Phil. 2:6–7). Second, what Paul means by sowing and reaping is that, as we give to others, God will "make [us] abound in every good work" (2 Cor. 9:8). The harvest is not more money or bigger businesses but "righteousness" and "thanksgiving to God" (9:10–11).

## The Pain-Free Life

Jesus often healed physical sickness and empowered his disciples to do the same (Matt. 4:23; 10:6–8). Indeed, after a series of Jesus's healings, Matthew cites Isaiah 53:4–5: "'He took our illnesses and bore our diseases'" (Matt. 8:17). Reflecting on this passage, Lindsay comments, "If [Christ] paid for our sicknesses, then we do not have to be sick."[4] Instead, "We must recognize sickness as a curse, the work of Satan and something to be banished from our lives."[5]

---

4. Lindsay, *Bible Secret of Divine Health*, 12.
5. Lindsay, *Bible Secret of Divine Health*, 5–6.

However, Jesus did not right all wrongs or relieve all pains during his first coming (Luke 4:16–21; 7:18–23). For instance, we know of him only raising three people from the dead (Mark 5:35–36, 41–43; Luke 7:12–15; John 11:38–46). There is, then, a tension we must hold in this "already-but-not-yet" period. Authors like Lindsay and Roberts fail to understand this tension, and thus they apply Scripture in unwise and unfaithful ways.

## Living in the Overlap of the Ages

Believers should boldly claim *all* of God's promises in Scripture. Every promise is truly ours already, but those we tangibly experience now are related to God's presence, power, and pleasure. All promises addressing physical, material provision will be realized fully only at the consummation (Rev. 21:4).

God may still, in view of his steadfast love (Ps. 31:7), bring our future hope into the present by means of a miracle. We must, then, not only pray that God would heal the suffering (Jas. 5:13–15) but also help the poor (Deut. 10:17–19; 1 John 3:17)—all for his glory and his kingdom's advance. God will relieve our suffering in his own way, but we can trust that he is working all things for our good (Rom. 8:28) and that he will one day restore creation.

# The New Testament's Application of Old Testament Promises to Christians

In grasping how Old Testament promises relate to us, we must not say, "We are part of the new covenant, and therefore old-covenant promises do not apply to us." In fact, the New Testament is very quick to cite Old Testament promises— assuming their lasting significance!

For example, Paul charges: "Never avenge yourselves, but leave it to the wrath of God, for it is written, 'Vengeance is mine, I will repay, says the Lord'" (Rom. 12:19). The apostle cites Deuteronomy 32:35, which Yahweh declares against all oppressors. Evidently, Paul believes that we can love our enemies when we trust that God will judge in the future. And we believe this because of an Old Testament promise.

Similarly, the author of Hebrews says, "Keep your life free from love of money, and be content with what you have, for he has said, 'I will never leave you nor forsake you'" (Heb. 13:5). Christians should not look to money for security *because* God has promised to be with us always! He draws on the pledge that Moses gave to Joshua and that Yahweh reaffirmed to Joshua just before Israel's conquest of Canaan (Deut. 31:8; Josh. 1:5). Somehow, Christians can and should legitimately use this promise to help us battle giants like covetousness in our own lives.

## Summary of the Need to Hope in Old Testament Promises

God's promises of provision and protection, including those from the Old Testament, are vital for helping us in our pursuit of godliness. Yet Christians need a framework for benefiting from Old Testament promises in a way that does not produce abuses, like those seen in prosperity teaching. We will now consider five principles that inform how Christians relate to Old Testament promises.

# The Christian's Connection to Old Testament Promises

Paul claims, "*All* the promises of God find their Yes in [Jesus]" (2 Cor. 1:20), but is he referring only to New Testament promises? After citing a list of Old Testament promises later in the epistle (6:16–18), he urges the Corinthians to pursue holiness "since we have these promises" (7:1). For Paul, Christians should hope in both Old Testament and New Testament promises, but only *in Jesus*. What follows are five principles that shape how the New Testament authors relate Old Testament promises to believers today.

## Christians Benefit from Old Testament Promises Only through Christ

In Galatians 3, Paul confronts claims that for Gentiles to become full inheritors of God's Old Testament promises, they need to submit to circumcision and the Mosaic law. In contrast, the apostle asserts that, while the old-covenant law served as a "guardian until Christ came …, now that [the age of] faith has come, we are no longer under a guardian" (Gal. 3:24–25). Furthermore, he stresses that only identifying with Christ Jesus by faith secures inheritance rights for Jew and Greek alike. All must receive "adoption as sons" (4:5).

Apparently with the promise of "lands" (plural) in Genesis 26:3 in mind, along with an allusion to 22:17–18, Paul says, "Now the promises were made to Abraham and to his offspring. It does not say, 'And to offsprings,' referring to many, but referring to one, 'And to your offspring,' who is Christ" (Gal. 3:16). Paul recognizes that Genesis places the hope of the world not on a people but on a person—not on a corporate Israel but on a representative, royal, messianic Deliverer. And now that this offspring has come, "if you are Christ's, then you are Abraham's offspring, heirs according to promise" (3:29). For Paul, only in Christ Jesus can anyone inherit the Old Testament's promised blessings. This is what Paul means when he declares that in Christ all of God's promises find their "yes" (2 Cor. 1:20).

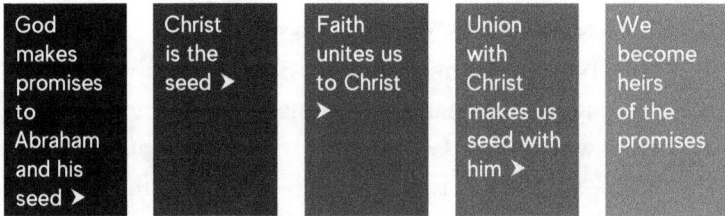

| God makes promises to Abraham and his seed ➤ | Christ is the seed ➤ | Faith unites us to Christ ➤ | Union with Christ makes us seed with him ➤ | We become heirs of the promises |
|---|---|---|---|---|

Figure 3.1. Old Testament Promises Reach Believers
Only through Christ[6]

## All Old-Covenant Curses Become New-Covenant Curses

With a heart full of hope, Moses wrote: "And the LORD your God will circumcise your heart and the heart of your offspring…. And the LORD your God will put all these curses on your foes and enemies who persecuted you" (Deut. 30:6–7). Notice here that in the age of new-covenant heart circumcision, which Paul says is being realized today (Rom. 2:29; Phil. 3:3), Yahweh will take Deuteronomy's curses and pour them out on the enemies of God's restored community. Whereas the original blessings include all levels of provision and protection (e.g., Deut. 28:1–14), the curses comprise the absolute removal of both (28:15–68). Thus, the old-covenant curses become new-covenant curses, which Yahweh brings not on the members of the new covenant but on their enemies. This is the hope to which Paul points when he recalls Yahweh's

---

6. John Piper, "Isaiah 41:10: Are the Old Testament Promises Made to Us?," Desiring God, 12 July 2016, http://www.desiringgod.org/labs/are-the-old-testament-promises-made-to-us.

promise in Deuteronomy 32:35 with these words: "Beloved, never avenge yourselves, but leave it to the wrath of God, for it is written, 'Vengeance is mine, I will repay, says the Lord'" (Rom. 12:19). As in the Abrahamic covenant, where Yahweh promised to curse anyone who dishonored the patriarch and those he represented (Gen. 12:3), so will Yahweh confront those who spurn his new-covenant community.

The New Testament displays new-covenant curses as warnings against permanently falling away from Christ and against all who oppose God and his people (see Matt. 25:31–46; Luke 6:20–26; 2 Tim. 2:12; Heb. 10:26–27). Those in Christ will not experience curse in a punitive way, for Christ bears upon himself God's curse against all believers (Gal. 3:13). While Christians still experience the Lord's fatherly discipline, no level of earthly discipline or consequence calls into question the eternal security of any believer (Rom. 5:9). Instead, new-covenant curses serve as a means of grace to those in Christ to generate within them reverent fear of God leading to greater holiness (see Rom. 2:4; 11:22; Heb. 6:1–9; 12:11; cf. Lev. 26:18, 21, 23, 27).

## In the New Covenant, Christians Inherit the Old Covenant's Original and Restoration Blessings

As already noted, Paul uses a string of Old Testament promises to motivate Christians to "not be unequally yoked with unbelievers" (2 Cor. 6:14). Significant here is the first citation: "What agreement has the temple of God with idols? For we are the temple of the living God; as God said, 'I will make my dwelling among them and walk among them, and I will be their God, and they shall be my people'" (6:16). Paul combines citations from an original old-covenant blessing (Lev.

26:11–12) and a restoration blessing (Ezek. 37:27). Figure 3.2 compares the texts.

| 2 Corinthians 6:16 (ESV) | |
|---|---|
| What agreement has the temple of God with idols? For we are the temple of the living God; as God said, "I will make my dwelling among them and walk among them, and I will be their God, and they shall be my people." | |
| **Leviticus 26:3, 11–12** | **Ezekiel 37:27** |
| **NETS** (translation from the Greek Old Testament) | **NETS** (translation from the Greek Old Testament) |
| If you walk by my ordinances and observe my commandments and do them, … I will place my tent [lit., "covenant"] among you, and my soul shall not abhor you. And I will walk about among you and will be your God, and you shall be for me a nation. | And my encamping shall be among them, and I will be a god for them, and they shall be my people. |
| **ESV** (translation from the Hebrew Old Testament) | **ESV** (translation from the Hebrew Old Testament) |
| If you walk in my statutes and observe my commandments and do them, … I will make my dwelling among you, and my soul shall not abhor you. And I will walk among you and will be your God, and you shall be my people. | My dwelling place shall be with them, and I will be their God, and they shall be my people. |

Figure 3.2. Paul's Use of the Old Testament in 2 Corinthians 6:16

Note that whereas the Greek of Ezekiel 37:27 reads "my dwelling shall be with them," Paul's wording is "I will make my dwelling among them." This difference suggests that the apostle is either quoting from memory or supplying his own rendering directly from the Hebrew. Regardless, the second half of the promise parallels closely the Greek translation. What is missing in Ezekiel, however, is any mention of God's "walking" among his people, and this suggests that, along with Ezekiel 37:27, Paul also has in mind the original Mosaic-covenant blessing of Leviticus 26:11–12.

Two conclusions follow from how Paul applies Old Testament promises in 2 Corinthians 6:16: (1) The restoration blessings of the old covenant include all the original blessings but in escalation and without the chance of loss. (2) Through Christ, the original old-covenant blessings *and* the restoration blessings have direct bearing on Christians. Paul draws together both texts, suggesting not only their close tie in the Old Testament but also that, along with the new-covenant restoration blessings, the original old-covenant blessings do indeed relate to believers.

## Christians Already Possess All Blessings of Their Inheritance but Will Enjoy Them Fully Only at Christ's Final Coming

Paul once declared, "Blessed be the God and Father of our Lord Jesus Christ, who has blessed us *in Christ* with every spiritual blessing …. *In him* you also … were sealed with the promised Holy Spirit, who is the guarantee of our inheritance until we acquire possession of it, to the praise of his glory" (Eph. 1:3, 13–14). "Every spiritual blessing" likely refers to all the blessings that Christ's Spirit secures for the saints, building upon our election, adoption, redemption, forgiveness, and sealing and including all his present provisions and all that we will enjoy when we gain our full inheritance (cf. 2 Cor. 1:20, 22; 1 Pet. 1:3–4).

All these blessings fulfill the Old Testament's end-time hopes associated with the promises of new-covenant restoration (e.g., Deut. 30:6; Isa. 53:11; Jer. 31:33–34; 32:40; Ezek. 36:27; 37:27; Dan. 9:24). Yet while *all* God's promises already find their "yes" for those in Christ (2 Cor. 1:20), a Christian's full enjoyment awaits the coming inheritance—truly now, fully later. As Paul put it in 2 Corinthians 1:22, "[God] has put his seal on us and given us his Spirit in our hearts as a guarantee."

## All True Christians Will Persevere and Enjoy Their Full Inheritance

Like other New Testament teachers (e.g., Matt. 5:8; 2 Cor. 7:1; Rev. 21:27), the author of Hebrews emphasizes that "without [holiness] no one will see the Lord" (Heb. 12:14). Persevering fruitfulness is a necessary condition to enjoy the future inheritance, for future judgment will be in accord with (though not based on) deeds we do in this life (Matt. 16:27; Rom. 2:6; 2 Cor. 5:10; 1 Pet. 1:17; Rev. 2:23; 20:12). Thus, Paul can stress, "If you live according to the flesh you will die, but if by the Spirit you put to death the deeds of the body, you will live" (Rom. 8:13).

These things stated, Paul clarifies that this new-covenant call to persevere is not like the old covenant's call to obey (Lev. 18:5). Speaking predominantly to the unregenerate, the old covenant charged Israel to pursue righteousness (Deut. 16:20), and it declared that they would only secure life and be counted righteous if they met all the covenant's demands (6:25; 8:1). Yet for Paul, "the very commandment that promised life proved to be death" (Rom. 7:10). Paul can thus declare that "Christ is the end of the law for righteousness to everyone who believes" (10:4), because by Christ's perfect obedience, God frees believers from sin's power (5:18–19; 8:1; Col. 2:14), declares us righteous (Rom. 5:9–10; 2 Cor. 5:21), and enables us to walk in newness of life (Rom. 6:4, 17, 22). In doing so, God generates persevering faith, hope, and love and thus makes certain the endurance of all new-covenant members.

## Summary of the Christian's Relationship to Old Testament Promises

At least five principles guided the New Testament authors when they related Old Testament promises to Christians: (1) Believers benefit from Old Testament promises only through Christ. (2) Old-covenant curses become new-covenant curses. (3) As part of the new covenant, Christians inherit the old covenant's original and restoration blessings. (4) Christians already possess all blessings of their inheritance but will enjoy them fully only at Christ's final coming. (5) All true Christians will persevere and enjoy their full inheritance. We will now overview four ways Christ serves as a lens for claiming Old Testament promises as Christians.

# How to Hope in Old Testament Promises through Christ

Yahweh's promises (old and new) are vital for Christians. If we fail to embrace Old Testament promises, we will lose three-fourths of the life-giving words of truth that our trustworthy God has given us. Yet we must appropriate them through Christ.

## "This Will Turn Out for My Deliverance"

Consider how Paul lived in hope by claiming promises that encouraged Job. The apostle opens his Philippian letter noting that he was in prison for Christ (Phil. 1:7) and that his imprisonment had itself advanced the gospel's spread (1:12–13). He then asserts: "Yes, and I will rejoice, for I know that through your prayers and the help of the Spirit of Jesus Christ *this will turn out for my deliverance*" (1:18–19, italics added).

With the italicized words in verse 19, Paul alludes to the Greek translation of Job 13:16, the only other place in Scripture where the clause occurs. Speaking out of his physical suffering, Job declared: "Though the Mighty One overpower me—in as much as he has begun—certainly I will speak and argue my case before him. And this will turn out for my deliverance" (author's translation, cf. NIV). Thus, just as Job anticipated that even death would not keep him from being saved, so Paul declared that his imprisonment would "turn out for [his] deliverance, … whether by life or by death" (Phil. 1:19–20). Like Job, Paul was convinced that he would be delivered, but this salvation could even come "by death."

Paul's sole hope for attaining Job's resurrection hope (3:11) was that he be found in Christ (3:9). The apostle, therefore, claims Job's promise through Jesus, whose own resurrection power (3:10) made both Job and Paul's hope possible. The very promises that kept Job fearing God were Paul's in Christ. And today they belong to all who are in Jesus.

## Four Ways Jesus Makes Every Promise "Yes"

Truly, *every* promise in Scripture is "Yes" in Christ (2 Cor. 1:20). Yet Jesus fulfills the Old Testament's promises in more than one way, and this means Christians cannot approach all Old Testament promises in the same manner. Believers must claim Scripture's promises using a salvation-historical framework that has Jesus at the center. Christ is the lens that clarifies and focuses the lasting significance of all God's promises for us (see fig. 3.3).

Old Testament Promises    Christ                    New Covenant Fulfillment

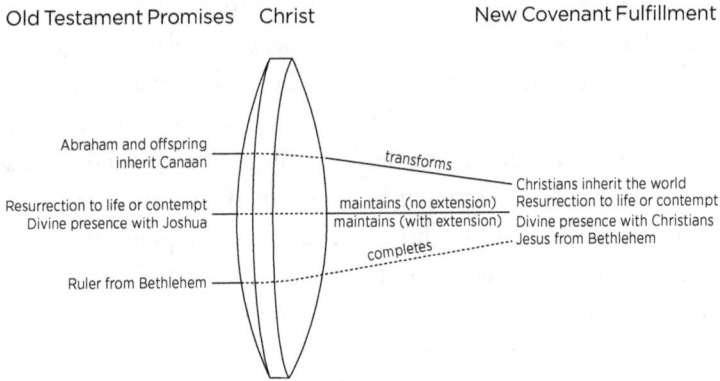

Figure 3.3. The Fulfillment of Old Testament Promises
through the Lens of Christ

## Christ Maintains Some Old Testament Promises with No Extension

Christ *maintains* certain promises without adding any further beneficiaries. For example, Daniel 12:2 envisioned a resurrection of some to everlasting life and of others to eternal contempt. Alluding to this passage, Jesus associated this same resurrection with his second coming: "An hour is coming when all who are in the tombs will hear [the Son of Man's] voice and come out, those who have done good to the resurrection of life, and those who have done evil to the resurrection of judgment" (John 5:28–29).

Christians should claim Daniel 12:2's promise of resurrection as our own. We do so, however, recognizing that we will only rise because Christ was first raised. "Christ has been raised from the dead, the firstfruits of those who have fallen asleep.... Christ the firstfruits, then at his coming those who belong to Christ" (1 Cor. 15:20, 23). This resurrection has an "already-and-not-yet" dimension, as the redeemed saints from both the Old Testament and New Testament epochs benefit from it. Jesus maintains the Old Testament promise without altering those profiting from it.

## Christ Maintains Some Old Testament Promises with Extension

When Christ fulfills some Old Testament promises, he extends the parties related to the promise. For instance, consider how Moses and Yahweh's promises to Joshua extend to Christians. Speaking to Joshua, Moses declared: "It is the LORD who goes before you. He will be with you; he will not leave you or forsake you" (Deut. 31:8). Later, Yahweh said to Joshua, "Just as I was with Moses, so I will be with you. I will not leave you or forsake you" (Josh. 1:5). And it is on this basis that the author of Hebrews writes: "Keep your life free from love of money, and be content with what you have, for he has said, '*I will never leave you nor forsake you*'" (Heb. 13:5, italics added).

In Hebrews, the Old Testament's wilderness and conquest narratives play an important role in magnifying Christ and the new covenant. Moses was faithful to God "as a servant," whereas Christ was faithful "as a son" (3:5). Some, like Joshua, believed that God was able to secure rest, but all others died because of unbelief (4:2). Later, Joshua led Israel into the promised land, but the rest he secured was only predictive of the greater rest that the more supreme Joshua (i.e., Jesus) would secure for all in him (4:8).

So, if the Lord was with the first Joshua and all who followed him, how much more can we be assured that he will be with those identify with the greater Joshua![7] The original promise God gave to one man bore implications for the whole community (Deut. 31:6), and now in the new covenant the same

---

7. William L. Lane, *Hebrews 9–13*, WBC 47B (Dallas: Word, 1991), 520.

promise expands to all who are in Christ. We already share in Christ Jesus (Heb. 3:14) but do not yet fully enjoy all that God promised (6:12). But because God has pledged, "I will never leave you nor forsake you" (13:5), Christians can rest secure knowing that we will one day fully enjoy the inheritance.

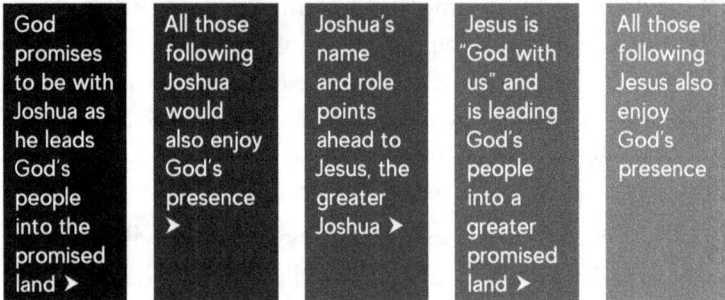

| God promises to be with Joshua as he leads God's people into the promised land ➤ | All those following Joshua would also enjoy God's presence ➤ | Joshua's name and role points ahead to Jesus, the greater Joshua ➤ | Jesus is "God with us" and is leading God's people into a greater promised land ➤ | All those following Jesus also enjoy God's presence |
|---|---|---|---|---|

Figure 3.4. God Maintains the Promise of His Presence
While Extending It to All in Christ

## Christ Himself Completes or Uniquely Realizes Some Old Testament Promises

Some Old Testament promises Christ has already completed or realized. For example, the prophet Micah predicted that a ruler in Israel would arise from Bethlehem (Mic. 5:2), and Christ exclusively fulfilled that promise at his birth (Matt. 2:6). Nevertheless, his birth was to spark a global return of "his brothers," and as king he would "shepherd his flock in the strength of the LORD," thus establishing lasting peace and enjoying a great name (Mic. 5:3–5). All these added promises continue to give comfort and hope to Christians, and Christ's birth in Bethlehem validates for us the certainty of his permanent and global exaltation.

Another example is Yahweh's promise to Solomon that, because he asked for wisdom rather than long life, riches, or punishment on his enemies, God would give him wisdom, riches, and honor (1 Kgs. 3:11–13). This promise is "Yes" in Christ in that on the cross Jesus purchased every divine bestowal of kindness, forbearance, and patience experienced in the realm of common grace (Gen. 8:20–21; Rom. 2:4; 3:25–26). Nevertheless, because the promise was contingent on one man's request and was related to his specific reign, the promise's specificity indicates that this is not a promise that every believer always enjoys. Instead, it was unique to Solomon himself, with others benefiting only from the wisdom, riches, and honor he himself enjoyed.

## Christ Transforms Some Old Testament Promises

At times, Jesus develops an Old Testament promise's makeup and audience. The land that Yahweh promised to Abraham and his offspring is of this kind (Gen. 13:15; 17:8; 48:4; Exod. 32:13). The patriarch would serve as a father of a single nation who would dwell in the land of Canaan (Gen. 17:8) and oversee an even broader geopolitical sphere (15:18). These realities are initially fulfilled in the Mosaic covenant (Exod. 2:24; 6:8; Deut. 1:8; 6:10; 9:5; 30:20; 34:4) and realized in the days of Joshua (Josh. 11:23; 21:43) and Solomon (1 Kgs. 4:20–21). Nevertheless, Genesis already foresees Abraham becoming the father of not just one nation but also *nations* (Gen. 17:4–6) and anticipates his influence reaching beyond the land (singular) to *lands* (plural) (26:3–4). This would happen when the royal offspring possesses the gate of his enemies and when all nations count themselves blessed in him (22:17b–18; 24:60).

In the new covenant, Christ transforms the type into the antitype by fulfilling the original land promise in himself and by extending it to the whole world through his people. In Paul's words, God promised "Abraham and his offspring that he would be heir of the *world*" (Rom. 4:13); at the consummation, the new earth will fully realize the antitype. While Christ maintains (without extension) Genesis's promises of the *antitypical* lands (plural), he does this by transforming the promises to Israel of the land (singular) as an "everlasting possession" (Gen. 17:8; 48:4). The nature of his fulfillment indicates that the land (singular) was but a type, which he transforms into the antitype, just as God had already foretold to the patriarchs.

# Conclusion

For Christians living in the overlap of the ages, God's promises provide motivation for growth in godliness (2 Pet. 1:4) and suffering with hope (Ps. 119:50). Often, God's promises are associated with life or death and conditioned on whether his covenant partner obeys. Whereas the old Mosaic covenant was conditional and revocable (and thus temporary considering Israel's disobedience), the Abrahamic covenant was conditional and irrevocable. This means that God would indeed realize all the promises but would do so only through an obedient Son. Representing Abraham and Israel, Jesus actively obeys and secures Old Testament promises for all who are in him. Christ maintains some promises without extension, maintains others with extension, completes some, and transforms others. Only through Christ do believers benefit from Old Testament promises. Old-covenant curses become new-covenant curses that God pours out on his enemies, and Christians today already possess the old covenant's original and restoration blessings but will enjoy them fully only when Christ's returns. All true believers will persevere and enjoy their full inheritance.

Four

# Living Well

## How Does Jesus Make Moses's Law Matter?

*"Do we then overthrow the law by this faith? By no means! On
the contrary, we uphold the law." (Rom. 3:31)*

The previous chapters addressed reading, seeing, and hoping
well. This chapter now considers how the Old Testament can
guide Christians to *living well.* Specifically, it seeks to help
Christians better understand their relationship to the Mosaic
law-covenant so that we can celebrate Christ's justifying and
sanctifying work more fully and receive God's intended guidance from the portrait of love found in the old-covenant law.
The Mosaic law does not *directly* bind the Christian in a legal
manner, but it is still profitable and instructive when read
through the lens of Christ. We will consider first the lasting
relevance of the Mosaic law and then the proposed three-fold
division of the law. After confronting three potentially dangerous perspectives on the Christian's relationship to the law,
we will then propose a model for discerning the law's lasting
relevance and look at four case studies, seeing how Jesus maintains certain laws with or without extension, transforms other
laws, and annuls some.

# The Christians' Connection to Moses's Law

How does the Old Testament law apply to Christians when so much has changed with Christ's coming, not least of which is that we are part of the new covenant and not the old? With a simple alliteration, Brian Rosner has captured well three principles that clarify the Christian's relationship to the Mosaic law. The biblical authors *repudiate* the old Mosaic law-covenant, *replace* Moses's law with the law of Christ, and then *reappropriate* the law of Moses through Christ.[1]

## Biblical Authors **Repudiate** the Mosaic Law-Covenant

By God's purposes, the Mosaic law multiplied transgression (Rom. 5:20; Gal. 3:19), exposed sin (Rom. 3:20), and brought wrath (4:15) to show that "one is justified by faith apart from works of the law" (3:28). Christians repudiate the Mosaic law-covenant, "for Christ is the end of the law for righteousness to everyone who believes" (10:4). "The law was our guardian until Christ came, in order that we might be justified by faith. But now that faith has come, we are no longer under a guardian" (Gal. 3:24–25). Thus, as the author of Hebrews declared: "In speaking of a new covenant, he makes the first one obsolete. And what is becoming obsolete and growing old is ready to vanish away" (Heb. 8:13). "The law made nothing perfect" (7:19), but in Christ we find a "better hope" (7:19), a "better covenant" (7:22), "better promises" (8:6), "better sacrifices" (9:23), "better possession" (10:34), a "better country" (11:16), a "better life" (11:35), and a "better word" (12:24).

---

1. Brian S. Rosner, *Paul and the Law: Keeping the Commandments of God*, NSBT 31 (Downers Grove, IL: InterVarsity Press, 2013), 208–9, 217–22.

## Biblical Authors **Replace** Moses's Law with the Law of Christ

Moses knew that Israel's system of worship was merely symbolic, suggesting that it would become obsolete when shadow moved to substance (Exod. 25:9, 40; Zech. 3:8–9; 6:12–13). Moses also affirmed the need for a better covenant—one in which Yahweh would accomplish for Israel what he did not accomplish with Moses (Deut. 29:4; 30:6, 8). Furthermore, the prophets longed for the day when God would teach every member of the blood-bought community (Isa. 54:13), write his law on their hearts (Jer. 31:33), and cause them to walk in his statutes (Ezek. 36:27). All these hopes have been realized through Christ's person and work (John 6:44–45; Rom. 2:14–15; 8:3–4; Col. 2:16–17).

As Christians, our "release from the law" (Rom. 7:6; cf. 6:14) in part means that the Mosaic law is no longer the direct authority and immediate judge of the conduct of God's people. The age of the Mosaic law-covenant has come to an end in Christ (10:4), so the law itself has ceased from having a central and determinative role among God's people (2 Cor. 3:4–18; Gal. 3:15–4:7). As a written legal code, not one of the 611 stipulations in the Mosaic law-covenant is directly binding on Christians. Instead, we are bound by the law of Christ (1 Cor. 9:20–21; Gal. 6:2), which is summarized in the call to love our neighbor and which James refers to as the perfect law (Jas. 1:25).

## Biblical Authors **Reappropriate** Moses's Law through Christ

While the New Testament authors highlight the Mosaic law's condemning nature and stress that believers are now under the law of Christ, they also apply Old Testament laws to

Christians based on Christ's justifying and sanctifying work (e.g., Eph. 6:2–3; 1 Tim. 5:17–18; 1 Pet. 1:15–16). As an illustration, in Romans 13:8–10, Paul urges believers, in view of God's mercies shown in Christ (Rom. 12:1; cf. chaps. 1–11), to fulfill the law by loving others. In this passage, Paul cites four commands associated with the Ten Commandments that focus directly on valuing those made in God's image. Yet by adding "any other commandment," he shows that love fulfills all Moses's directives, even those beyond the Decalogue.

Although Moses's law does not *directly* bind Christians legally, we do not throw out the law itself. As Moses himself foresaw, God's people would turn and "obey the voice of the LORD and keep all his commandments" in the day of heart circumcision (Deut. 30:8). Along with *repudiating* the old covenant and *replacing* its law with the law of Christ, then, Christians must *reappropriate* Moses's instruction (1) as a testimony to God's character and values, (2) as prophecy that anticipates the gospel of Jesus, and (3) as wisdom intended to guide new-covenant saints in our pursuit of God.

## Moses's Law Reveals God's Character and Values

The Mosaic law expresses God's character and values. Yahweh asserted, "You shall ... be holy, for I am holy" (Lev. 19:2), and the way Israel would fulfill this charge was by heeding God's words (Exod. 19:5–6; Num. 15:40). Paul stressed that the law is "the embodiment of knowledge and truth" (Rom. 2:20) and that "the commandment is holy, righteous, and good" (7:12). Peter, too, asserted, "As he who called you is holy, you also be holy in all your conduct, since it is written, 'You shall be holy, for I am holy'" (1 Pet. 1:15–16). Moses's law signals what Yahweh values and hates, what he delights in and detests. Christians learn about the character of God through Moses's

law, and this in turn can clarify what it means to image him
faithfully (Gen. 1:26–28).

## Moses's Law Anticipates the Gospel Concerning Christ

Jesus stressed that he came not "to abolish the Law and the
Prophets" but "to fulfill them" (Matt. 5:17). By "fulfill," he
meant in part that he supplies the end-times actualization of
all the Old Testament predicted.[2] Thus, "all the Prophets and
the Law prophesied until John" (Matt. 11:13), and the very
"gospel of God ... concerning his Son" was "promised beforehand through his prophets in the holy Scriptures" (Rom.
1:1–3). Jesus stood as the goal and end of the Old Testament's
hopes, pictures, and patterns.

As the last Adam (1 Cor. 15:45), the representative of Israel
(Isa. 49:1–6; Matt. 21:9; Luke 1:32–33), the true Passover lamb
(John 1:29; 1 Cor. 5:7), and the true temple (John 2:21), Christ is
the substance of all old-covenant shadows (Col. 1:16–17; Heb.
8:5; 10:1). His role as teacher and covenant mediator also fulfills
Moses's own hopes for a covenant-mediating "prophet" like
him—one who would know God face to face, who would per-
form great wonders, and to whom people would listen (Deut.
18:15–19; 34:10–12; cf. Luke 7:16; Acts 3:22–26).

## Moses's Law Guides Christians in Love and Wise Living

The "law of Christ" that we live out (Isa. 42:4; 1 Cor. 9:21) is
the law of love as fulfilled and taught by Jesus, which is the
end-times realization of Moses's law. Jesus said that "all the
Law and the Prophets" depend on the commands to love God

---

2. Tom Wells and Fred G. Zaspel, *New Covenant Theology: Description, Definition, Defense* (Frederick,
MD: New Covenant Media, 2002), 115.

and neighbor (Matt. 22:37–40). Paul added that "the whole law is fulfilled in one word: 'You shall love your neighbor as yourself'" (Gal. 5:14). Significantly, every commandment, not just a "moral" subset of the law, is fulfilled in the call to love (Rom. 13:8–10).

In both the old and new covenants, then, love is *what* God's people are to do. All the other commandments simply clarify *how* to do it. From this perspective, while the Mosaic law does not directly or immediately guide Christians, it does show us how deeply and pervasively we should love God and neighbor.

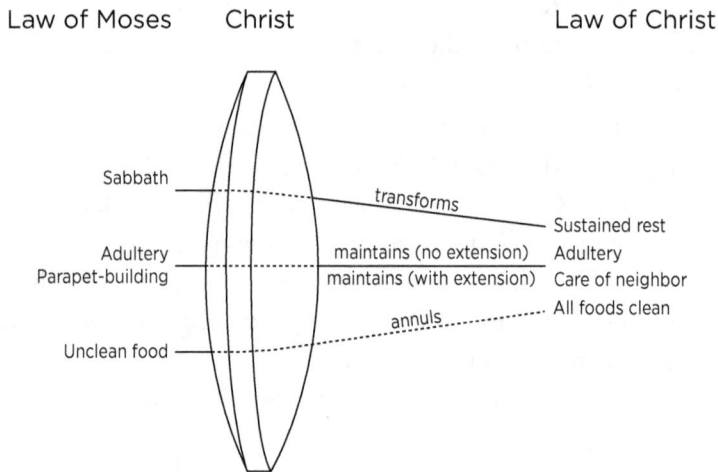

Figure 4.1. The Law's Fulfillment through the Lens of Christ

## Four Ways Christ Fulfills Moses's Law

Jesus is the lens that clarifies how to rightly appropriate the law of Moses, and he alone supplies the power to obey it. When Moses's instruction is viewed through this lens (see fig. 4.1), some laws appear unchanged, whereas others hit the lens and

get "bent" in various ways. Jesus's coming maintains (with
and without extension), transforms, and annuls various laws.

Another way to grasp how Christians should relate to Old
Testament law is to visualize two riverbanks separated at vary-
ing distances by water (see fig. 4.2). The two sides symbolize
the old- and new-covenant laws, and Jesus is the "bridge" over
which we must move from one side to the other. Our distance
from the Mosaic legislation changes depending on the nature of
the law in question. Thus, some laws (e.g., prohibitions against
murder and adultery) are so similar that the distance seems
almost nonexistent, but other laws (e.g., relating to food laws
and the Sabbath) disclose substantial distance.

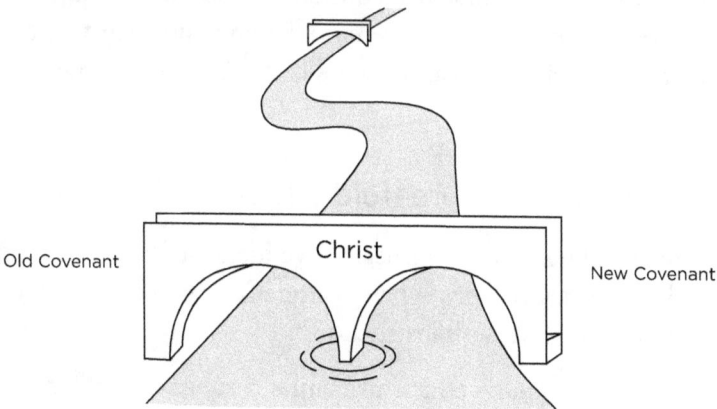

Figure 4.2. The Law's Fulfillment over the Bridge of Christ

## Summary of the Christian's Connection to Moses's Law

Jesus and the New Testament authors *repudiate* the Mosaic
law-covenant, *replace* Moses's law with the law of Christ, and
*reappropriate* Moses's law through Christ. They do this to
give us glimpses of God's character and to guide believers in
wisdom and love. None of Moses's law is directly binding on

God's people today in a legal or regulatory way (Rom. 7:4; Gal. 3:24–25). Nevertheless, it continues to impact us through Christ in both revelatory and pedagogical ways. Christ is like a lens, and through him (and his New Testament revelation) we can discern whether he maintains, transforms, or annuls any given law.

# Other Views on the Christian and Old Testament Law

There are alternative proposals to how Moses's law relates to Christians. We first will consider the common distinction between moral, civil, and ceremonial law and then will confront three dangerous approaches to the law that followers of Christ must avoid.

## Assessing the Threefold Division of the Law

Historically, many evangelicals have identified three theological categories of laws when considering the contemporary importance of Moses's instruction:

- *Moral laws*—ethical principles that are eternally applicable, regardless of covenant
- *Civil laws*—applications of the moral law to Israel's political and social structures
- *Ceremonial laws*—symbolic requirements related to religious rituals and cult worship

Many covenant theologians believe that the moral laws remain binding on Christians today, whereas the civil and ceremonial laws are no longer applicable. In contrast, Christian reconstructionists assert that, because civil laws apply moral laws situationally, they too carry over through Christ and are to guide all nations and states (not just the church).

While these approaches helpfully celebrate Christ as the substance of all Old Testament shadows (Col. 2:16–17; Heb. 8:5–7) and that his coming alters some laws more than others, neither model satisfies the biblical testimony concerning Moses's law. Against both approaches, as noted above, *none* of the Mosaic covenant is directly binding on Christians today (Rom. 10:4; 1 Cor. 9:20–21; Gal. 3:24–25), but *all* of it is still significant as revelation, prophecy, and wisdom when mediated through Christ (Matt. 5:17–19). Furthermore, Scripture views *all* the law as a single entity, *all* the law to be moral in nature, and *all* the law to have devotional benefit for believers.

## The Law as a Singular Entity

The Old Testament identifies types of laws based on content, but it never distinguishes laws in the way the threefold division proposes. Leviticus 19, for example, shows little distinction between laws, mixing calls to love one's neighbor (vv. 11–12, 17–18) with various commands related to family (vv. 3a, 29), worship (vv. 3b–8, 26–28, 30–31), business (vv. 9–10, 13b, 19a, 23–25, 34b–36), care (vv. 9–10, 13–14, 33–34), disputes (vv. 15–16, 35a), and rituals (v. 19b).

Furthermore, the New Testament regularly speaks of the law as a unit. In Romans 13:9, for instance, the call to love one's neighbor synthesizes not just a group of moral laws but every commandment, including the proposed civil and ceremonial legislation. Jesus and James, too, spoke broadly of the law (Matt. 5:19; Jas. 2:10). Paul stressed that the law brought curse to all (Gal. 3:10), that we are no longer under the law-covenant in Christ (3:24–25), and that "every man who accepts circumcision ... is obligated to keep the whole law" (5:3).

## The "Moral" Nature of All Laws

The "civil" laws illustrate moral principles worked out in Isra-elite culture. Furthermore, the "ceremonial" laws demonstrate moral elements through symbolism, and even the Ten Com-mandments, often deemed the premier example of moral law, contain many culturally bound features:

- The prologue identifies Israel as a people redeemed from Egyptian slavery (Deut. 5:6).
- The idolatry command assumes a religious system including carved images (5:8).
- The Sabbath command presumes ancient Near Eastern bond service, geographically limited animals, and cities with gates (5:14).[3]

This list should caution those who want to distinguish civil or ceremonial laws from moral because of their temporal boundedness.

## The Benefit of All Old Testament Law

Most theologians espousing the threefold division of the law affirm the lasting value of *all* Scripture. However, this division has led many to see the Book of the Covenant (Exod. 21–23) and Leviticus as having little lasting relevance. Yet Jesus and Paul affirmed Exodus's prohibitions against reviling parents (Matt. 15:4) and leaders (Acts 23:5), Paul drew pastoral insight from Leviticus's instructions on temple service (1 Cor. 9:13–14), and Peter called believers to holiness *because* God called for it in Leviticus (1 Pet. 1:15–17). "All Scripture ... is profit-able" for Christians (2 Tim. 3:16), and we align most closely

---

3. David A. Dorsey, "The Law of Moses and the Christian: A Compromise," *Journal of the Evangelical Theological Society* 34 (1991): 330.

with the Bible when we emphasize how the *entire* law still matters for Christians, though not all in the same way.

## Dangerous Applications of Old Testament Law

Before learning how to apply Moses's law through Jesus and supplying some extended case studies, we must consider three destructive approaches to Old Testament law: (1) legalism, (2) antinomianism, and (3) anti-Old Testament thought.

### Legalism

*Legalism* is operative when people trust in their own doing to enjoy right standing with God (Luke 18:9; Gal. 3:3). Foundational to the very nature of the old-covenant law was Yahweh's claim, "If a person does them [i.e., my statutes and rules], he shall live by them" (Lev. 18:5). Because God gave the law to a mostly unregenerate people, their pursuit of righteousness by works and not by faith resulted in their ruin (Rom. 7:10; 9:30–32).

As rightly affirmed during the Reformation, foundational to all biblical doctrine is that justification before God comes by grace *alone* through faith *alone* in Christ *alone*. And we become legalists if we ever ground our justification in anything other than Christ's perfect obedience *alone*. "Therefore, as one trespass led to condemnation for all men, so one act of righteousness leads to justification and life for all men. For as by the one man's disobedience the many were made sinners, so by the one man's obedience the many will be made righteous" (5:18–19).

## Antinomianism

In the New Testament, *nomos* is the Greek term for "law," so *antinomian* means "no law." Antinomians, then, are those who claim that God's rules need not influence Christians' daily ethics. In contrast, Paul stressed that he was not "outside the law of God but under the law of Christ" (1 Cor. 9:21) and that what counts is neither circumcision nor uncircumcision but "keeping the commandments of God" (7:19).

Long ago, the Westminster theologians highlighted, "Faith, thus receiving and resting on Christ and his righteousness, is the alone instrument of justification: yet it is not alone in the person justified, but is ever accompanied with all other saving graces, is no dead faith, but worketh by love."[4] It is from this framework that, after forgiving the sin of the woman caught in adultery, Jesus commanded, "Go, and from now on sin no more" (John 8:11). Similarly, Peter urged, "As obedient children, do not be conformed to the passions of your former ignorance, but as he who called you is holy, you also be holy in all your conduct, since it is written, 'You shall be holy, for I am holy'" (1 Pet. 1:14–16). Clearly, antinomianism is not an option for Christians.

## Anti-Old Testament Thought

In his book *Irresistible*, Andy Stanley claims that one of the church's greatest problems today is "our incessant habit of reaching back into the old-covenant concepts, teachings, sayings, and narratives."[5] He stresses that we should call the Old Testament the "Hebrew Bible" and the New Testament the "Christian Bible,"[6] even warning against too quickly finding Christ in the Old Testament, lest we be among those

4. Westminster Confession of Faith 11.2.
5. Andy Stanley, *Irresistible: Reclaiming the New That Jesus Unleashed for the World* (Grand Rapids: Zondervan, 2018), 90.
6. Stanley, *Irresistible*, 280.

who have "hijacked" the Jewish Scriptures by "ignoring the original context" and by "retrofitting them as Christian Scripture."[7] Stanley also assumes that none of Moses's law matters today: "Thou shalt not obey the Ten Commandments," he says.[8]

Stanley rightly affirms that Christians are part of the new covenant, not the old, and that Christ stands as the end of old-covenant worship laws.[9] Nevertheless, he overlooks the fact that Jesus maintains some laws and transforms others. Stanley also overlooks the facts that Jesus and Paul's only Bible was what we call the Old Testament, that they saw it pointing to the Messiah and his work (Luke 24:44–47; Acts 26:22–23), and that they recognized the whole Old Testament to be Christian Scripture (Rom. 15:4; 1 Cor. 10:11; 1 Pet. 1:12). Stanley treats the Old Testament as if Jesus came to "abolish" rather than "fulfill" it (Matt. 5:17), and he fails to help people understand how the initial three-fourths of Christian Scripture is "profitable for teaching, for reproof, for correction, and for training in righteousness" (2 Tim. 3:16).

## Summary of Alternative Approaches to the Law

Many Christians distinguish between moral, civil, and ceremonial laws and then view only the moral or only the moral and civil as applying to Christians. Both approaches miss that no old-covenant legislation directly binds believers today, that all of Moses's law still serves Christians through Jesus, but only insofar as he maintains, transforms, or annuls the various laws. While principles of love and justice in Moses's law also carry over into governments today, Christ's law binds the church

---

7. Stanley, *Irresistible*, 156.
8. Stanley, *Irresistible*, 136.
9. Stanley, *Irresistible*, 17–65.

and not the state. Finally, legalism, antinomianism, and the
view that the Old Testament no longer applies to Christians
are all dangerous teachings, for they compromise Christ's
saving work.

| Criminal Laws | Laws governing offenses that put the welfare of the whole community at risk (i.e., crimes); the offended party is the state or national community, and, therefore, the punishment is on behalf of the whole community in the name of the highest state authority, which in Israel meant Yahweh. <u>Examples</u>: Kidnapping, homicide, false prophecy, witchcraft, adultery, and rape. |
|---|---|
| Civil Laws | Laws governing private disputes between citizens or organizations in which the public authorities are appealed to for judgment or called upon to intervene; the offended party is not the state or national community. <u>Examples</u>: Accidental death and assault, theft, destruction of property, limited family issues like premarital unchastity, post-divorce situations, and the mistreatment of slaves. |
| Family Laws | Non-civil, domestic laws governing the Israelite household. <u>Examples</u>: Marriage, inheritance, the redemption of land and persons, family discipleship, and the care of slaves. |
| Cultic/ Ceremonial Laws | Laws governing the visible forms and rituals of Israel's religious life or ceremonies. <u>Examples</u>: The sacred sacrifice, the sacred calendar, and various sacred symbols like the tabernacle, priesthood, and ritual purity that distinguished Israel from the nations and provided parables of more fundamental truths about God and relating to him. |
| Compassion Laws | "Laws" dealing with charity, justice, and mercy toward others; these laws cannot be brought to court, but God knows the heart. <u>Examples</u>: Protection and justice for the weak, impartiality, generosity, and respect for persons and property. |

Figure 4.3. Types of Laws by Content

# How Jesus Maintains Some Old Testament Laws

Having evaluated how the Bible relates Old Testament law to Christians and having considered some of the errors and dangers in alternative approaches, we will now overview a three-step process for applying Old Testament law today (see fig. 4.3). After this, we will look at four case-studies on commands that Christ's new-covenant law maintains, transforms, or annuls.

## A Method for Applying Old Testament Law

The following three-step process will help believers faithfully assess through Christ and for Christ the lasting significance of Moses's law today.

### Establish the Law's Original Meaning and Application

*Categorize the Type of Law:* What type or kind of command are you assessing—criminal, civil, family, cultic/ceremonial, or compassion law? At stake here is the law's content, not form (e.g., foundational principles [apodictic] vs. circumstantial applications [casuistic]).

*Establish the Law's Original Meaning and Significance:* Assess the makeup of the law in its original context. Clarify its social function and relative status. Is it central or peripheral to the dominant themes and objectives we find in the rest of the material? Is it a primary expression of Yahweh's values and priorities, or is it more secondary, reinforcing and supplying an example of a more primary law?

*Consider the Law's Original Purpose:* What role did Yahweh intend the law to have in Israelite society? Ask the following: Who? What? When? Where? Why? How? How often? To what extent?

## Determine the Law's Theological Importance

*Clarify What the Law Tells Us About God:* What does the law disclose about Yahweh's character, desires, values, concerns, or standards? We learn about the unchanging God through his law, and meditating on Moses's law should move us to worship the Lord and to recognize and grieve over lawlessness as a direct affront to his person. It should also move us to celebrate his provision of Christ as the perfect law keeper and righteousness supplier.

*Evaluate How Christ Fulfills the Law and Consider Its Impact on Application:* Christ's person, teaching, and work display the call to love God and neighbor, and Jesus fulfills the law not only in the way he perfectly obeyed it but also in the way that he is the substance of all old-covenant shadows (Col. 2:16–17). As we consider how Moses's law informs the law of Christ, some new-covenant instructions look identical to Moses's teaching, whereas others are maintained with extension, transformed, or annulled. Because the various types of laws are mixed in the Torah, we must deal with each law on its own.

*State the Love Principle Behind the Law:* If indeed love is what God called the people to do and all the other commandments clarify how to do it (Matt. 7:12; 22:37–40; Rom. 13:8, 10; Gal. 5:14), we should be able to boil down every law into a *principle of love.* In detail, complete the following statement for every law: The call to love God or neighbor means / implies / impacts / necessitates _____.

### Summarize the Law's Lasting Significance

Here we preserve both the portrait of God and the love principle behind the law but change the context, all in view of Christ's work. God's nature is unchanging, but his purposes progress over time. Furthermore, a proper approach to Old Testament law must account for the pattern Christ set for believers and the power he supplies through his victory and his Spirit.

## Case Study #1: The Law on Parapet Building Maintained with Extension

Our first example of applying Moses's law is a "slow-pitch, easy-hitter." It illustrates how some laws get extended into new spheres as times and cultures change.

> When you build a new house, you shall make a parapet for your roof, that you may not bring the guilt of blood upon your house, if anyone should fall from it. (Deut. 22:8)

### Establish the Original Meaning and Application of Deuteronomy 22:8

Flat roofs are common throughout the Middle East, as the roof supplies an extra living space. A parapet is the low wall that surrounds the roof and that protects people from falling off. Hence, a homeowner needs to build his house with a parapet to guard against another's death. The law's conditional nature suggests it stands as a secondary application of the more fundamental principle of compassion. Its main purpose was to prevent domestic casualties brought about by mishap or negligence.

## Determine the Theological Importance of Deuteronomy 22:8

God treasures when humans display his image, and he calls his people to value those made in his image. In Deuteronomy 22:8, Yahweh graciously warns against dangers that could result in injury to others. Similarly, the "golden rule" that Christ advocated (Matt. 7:12) is evident in our passage, and it requires that Christ's followers today love others in the most practical of ways, including how we ready our living space for guests. Hence, *the call to love others means we will remove potential dangers and make our living environment safe.*

## Summarize the Lasting Significance of Deuteronomy 22:8

All homeowners bear the responsibility to care for their guests' well-being. While many societies do not have houses with parapets, Deuteronomy 22:8 is naturally extended to include, say, building a fence around a pool, placing a protective gate above a stairwell, or salting a sidewalk after an ice storm. Love for neighbor is to impact even the littlest details of daily life. For an example of this type of usage in the New Testament, see Paul's application of Deuteronomy 25:4's principle of not muzzling an ox in 1 Corinthians 9:7–11 and 1 Timothy 5:17–18.

# Case Study #2: The Law on Crossdressing Maintained without Extension

Much of the world is amid a gender-identity crisis, and the brokenness it is causing is tragic. When read through the lens of Jesus, Deuteronomy 22:5 speaks to this issue.[10]

---

10. What follows is abridged from Jason S. DeRouchie, "Confronting the Transgender Storm: New Covenant Reflections on Deuteronomy 22:5," *Journal for Biblical Manhood and Womanhood* 21, no. 1 (2016): 58–69.

A woman shall not wear a man's garment, nor shall a man put on a woman's cloak, for whoever does these things is an abomination to the LORD your God. (Deut. 22:5)

## Establish the Original Meaning and Application of Deuteronomy 22:5

We should note three features about this prohibition. First, given its use of *géber* ("man") rather than *'îš* ("man, husband"), the prohibition is not restricted to husbands and wives but includes the broader society. Second, certain articles of clothing, such as a man's "garment" (*kᵉlî*) and a woman's "cloak" (*śimlâ*), distinguished men and women in Israelite culture. Third, the fact that cross-dressing is an "abomination" highlights the gravity of the offense and associates it with idolatry (Deut. 13:14; 17:4), witchcraft (18:12), and dishonest gain (25:16), which could relate to criminal, civil, or family law.

In this light, Deuteronomy 22:5 appears less a core principle and more a secondary application of more fundamental truths—that there are two biological sexes (male and female) and that one's biological sex should govern one's gender identity *and* expression. As for the purpose of the law, it appears to maintain divinely created gender distinctions.

## Determine the Theological Importance of Deuteronomy 22:5

Yahweh is passionate about displaying right order in his world. This is the essence of his righteousness, and maintaining gender distinctions is an important part of this order. Moreover, Christ and his apostles continued to distinguish men from women. Indeed, Jesus affirmed the male and female distinction (Matt. 19:4; Mark 10:6) and perfectly exemplified maleness in the way he deeply respected femaleness (see, e.g., Matt. 5:27–32; Mark

5:25–43; Luke 7:36–8:3; John 7:53–8:11). In addition, gender distinctions will continue until the consummation (Eph. 5:22–33; 1 Tim. 3:4–5), and even if earthly marriage will end (Matt. 22:30), there is no reason to think that gender distinctions will alter in the new heavens and new earth (cf. Rev. 21:24). According to Deuteronomy 22:5, then, *loving others and God means that people will maintain a gender identity that aligns with their biological sex and that they will express their gender in a way that never leads to confusion.*

## Summarize the Lasting Significance of Deuteronomy 22:5

Deuteronomy 22:5 helps us recognize the appropriate path for gender expression and the sinfulness of gender confusion, which includes cross-dressing and transgender practice. Western culture still distinguishes men's and women's clothing, even if women can at times wear slacks, collars, and ties with no one questioning their femaleness. What was at stake in Moses's law was gender confusion, and it is from this perspective that our outward apparel matters.

Deuteronomy 22:5 focuses on adults and addresses gender *expression* and *confusion*. As such, it would not directly dissuade a girl from sporting a mustache in a theatre production or a boy putting on a girl's dress at home. No viewer of this "child's play" would be confused regarding the child's gender. Nevertheless, we must be cautious, because we are always shaping our children, and we live in a society that acts as though gender is a matter of choice rather than providence. This perspective is abominable, and Deuteronomy 22:5 speaks directly against it.

May the church care deeply for the violators and the violated in the present gender-identity crisis. We need to help those struggling with identity to find a new identity in Christ, and we need to help those who have been hurt to find the healing that only Jesus brings. He alone is Savior. He alone is Healer.

## Case Study #3: The Law of the Sabbath Transformed

Considering the Sabbath command in Deuteronomy 5:12–15 will show us how important it is to consider Christ's fulfillment, which in this instance fully transforms the law and guides those strong in faith in the path of love.

> Observe the Sabbath day, to keep it holy, as the LORD your God commanded you. Six days you shall labor and do all your work, but the seventh day is a Sabbath to the LORD your God. On it you shall not do any work, you or your son or your daughter or your male servant or your female servant, or your ox or your donkey or any of your livestock, or the sojourner who is within your gates, that your male servant and your female servant may rest as well as you. You shall remember that you were a slave in the land of Egypt, and the LORD your God brought you out from there with a mighty hand and an outstretched arm. Therefore the LORD your God commanded you to keep the Sabbath day. (Deut. 5:12–15)

### Establish the Original Meaning and Application of Deuteronomy 5:12–15

In Deuteronomy's version of the Ten Commandments (or Ten Words), discourse features create five groupings of long and short commands that highlight the centrality of the Sabbath within the old covenant:

| Word 1 | **No other gods** | Deut. 5:6–10 | Command Grouping #1: Long |
| Word 2 | **Bear Yahweh's name** | Deut. 5:11 | Command Grouping #2: Short |
| Word 3 | **Observe the Sabbath** | Deut. 5:12–15 | Command Grouping #3: Long |
| Word 4 | **Honor parents** | Deut. 5:16 | Command Grouping #4: Short |
| Words 5–10 | **Love neighbor** | Deut. 5:17–21 | Command Grouping #5: Long |

Figure 4.4. The Centrality of the Sabbath in the Decalogue

The Sabbath was central to Israel's identity and, therefore, stood as the old covenant's "sign" (Exod. 31:13, 17). Michael Fox notes three common functions of covenant signs in the Old Testament:[11]

1. *Validation signs* demonstrated or proved the truth of something.

2. *Symbol signs* represented a future reality (whether curse or blessing) by virtue of resemblance or association.

3. *Cognition signs* aroused knowledge of something by identifying or reminding.

The Sabbath served first as a cognition sign and then as a symbol sign. It distinguished Israel from the rest of the world and symbolically reminded them of their calling to serve as the agents through whom right order and peace with God under his sovereignty would be enjoyed on a global scale (ultimately through their Messiah). That is, Israel's 6 + 1 pattern of life

---

11. Michael V. Fox, "The Sign of the Covenant: Circumcision in the Light of Priestly 'ôt Etiologies, *Revue biblique* 81 (1974): 562–63.

set a missional, goal-oriented structure to their existence, such
that working six days and resting on one recalled their mission
to see Sabbath rest realized once again throughout the world.

The entire purpose of the old covenant was symbolized in
the Sabbath, and its importance is highlighted by the fact that
breaking it was a criminal offense (Num. 15:32–36). While Sabbath was part of criminal law, its symbolism (like that of the
dietary laws addressed in the next case study) suggests that it
was also ceremonial law.

### Determine the Theological Importance of Deuteronomy 5:12–15

The Sabbath command teaches us many things about God:
(a) Yahweh shows no partiality. (b) Yahweh gives his people
opportunities to test their trust and to develop their depen-
dence. (c) Yahweh is passionate to display right order in his
world, wherein he is exalted as Sovereign over all things.

Jesus came at the climax of God's redemptive story.
Through his perfect obedience unto death followed by his resurrection, he represented a remnant from humanity in general
and of Israel in particular. Fulfilling Israel's pattern of Sabbath
rest, Jesus restored right order to reality, allowing members of
the new creation to enjoy peace with God and ultimate rest
once again. He, thus, charges, "Come to me, all who labor and
are heavy laden, and I will give you rest" (Matt. 11:28). Then,
directly following this assertion, he allows his disciples to pluck
grain on the Sabbath and calls himself "lord of the Sabbath"
(12:8). Jesus's redeeming work fulfilled Israel's global Sabbath
mission and inaugurated the end-times Sabbath rest for the
world.

The love principle standing behind Deuteronomy 5:12–15 is this: *Loving God and neighbor required carrying out the 6 + 1 pattern of life as a witness to the kingdom hope of ultimate rest.*

## Summarize the Lasting Significance of Deuteronomy 5:12–15

The old-covenant Sabbath command reminds believers today of God's gift of rest, by which God graciously counters workaholism and nurtures deeper levels of trust in him (Ps. 127:2). Nevertheless, Jesus fulfilled Israel's Sabbath pattern, bringing the goal of the 6+1 cycles to realization. He, indeed, is the substance of Israel's Sabbath (Col. 2:16–17). Thus, his coming brings sustained spiritual rest for every believer all the time, which means that all days are holy and that one day is not more precious than another (Rom. 14:5). We must maintain a pattern of corporate worship (Heb. 10:25), and the Lord's day of resurrection—Sunday—is a natural time for this (Acts 20:7; 1 Cor. 16:2) due to its end-times significance as the day on which God in Christ ignited his new creation (Rom. 6:4; 1 Cor. 15:20; Rev. 14:4). Nevertheless, corporate worship on another day of the week is not sin, nor is it necessarily wrong to weed your garden, study for an exam, or engage in sports on a Sunday—so long as you don't replace grace (1 Cor. 15:10; Phil. 2:12–13; Col. 3:17, 23). Through Christ, God has transformed the Sabbath in a way that believers now enjoy his sovereign rest seven days a week.

# Case Study #4: The Law Distinguishing Unclean Animals Annulled

This final illustration of applying Old Testament law to Christians addresses a command that Christ's coming annuls—yet in such a way that we can still benefit from it.

You shall therefore separate the clean beast from the unclean, and the unclean bird from the clean. You shall not make yourselves detestable by beast or by bird or by anything with which the ground crawls, which I have set apart for you to hold unclean. You shall be holy to me, for I the LORD am holy and have separated you from the peoples, that you should be mine. (Lev. 20:25–26)

## Establish the Original Meaning and Application of Leviticus 20:25-26

Pre-fall, God's prohibition of eating from a certain tree supplied a context for humankind to mature in wisdom (Gen. 2:17; cf. 3:5). The first couple disobeyed, and the result was that God cursed the world and marked certain creatures as unclean (7:2–3). Originally, the clean-unclean distinction appears to have only guided sacrifices (8:20; 9:3–4). However, it eventually served to distinguish God's people from the nations (Lev. 20:25–26). Either way, it was vital within Israel's religious life (10:10).

Unclean creatures shared some commonality with the serpent's curse or death-causing activities. Because Israel's neighbors were the serpent's offspring (see Gen. 3:15), the meaning Israel associated with unclean animals paralleled God's perspective of the nations. Accordingly, Yahweh's prohibition against eating unclean animals symbolically distinguished Israel from its neighbors. It also allowed Israel to point the world to Yahweh as the only Savior who could overcome curse with blessing (Gen. 12:3; 22:18).

## Determine the Theological Importance of Leviticus 20:25-26

God is holy, and all should see and celebrate this. John Hartley notes that, within the old covenant, dietary restrictions "made the Israelites conscious at every meal that they were to order their lives to honor the holy God with whom they were in covenant."[12] So, for example, the prohibition against eating pork served to heighten the Israelites' awe of Yahweh and to distinguish them from those outside the covenant.

With the progression of salvation history, however, Jesus has declared "all foods clean" (Mark 7:19). Accordingly, it is not what goes into peoples' mouths but what comes out of their hearts that defiles them (7:18–23). Similarly, the Lord gave Peter a vision of unclean animals, commanded him to "kill and eat," and then asserted, "What God has made clean, do not call common" (Acts 10:10–15). This instruction proved to Peter that God was now welcoming any from the nations who would fear and obey him (10:34–35). Within the original Old Testament context, then, *loving one's neighbor by not eating unclean food means that Israel was to display God's holy animosity toward sin and the curse even in their diet.*

## Summarize the Lasting Significance of Leviticus 20:25-26

When considering how eating today relates to loving our neighbors, we must view it from two angles. First, love of neighbor means that those who are strong in faith and who feel free to eat anything must be careful not to cause those who are weaker in faith and who choose to abstain from certain foods to stumble. As Paul writes, "Food will not commend

---

12. J. E. Hartley, "Holy and Holiness, Clean and Unclean," in *Dictionary of the Old Testament: Pentateuch*, ed. T. Desmond Alexander and David W. Baker (Downers Grove, IL: InterVarsity, 2003), 429.

us to God. We are no worse off if we do not eat, and no better off if we do. But take care that this right of yours does not somehow become a stumbling block to the weak" (1 Cor. 8:8–9; cf. Rom. 14:2, 13–15).

Second, love of neighbor means that we will *not* stop proclaiming that Christ has triumphed on our behalf, opening the door for all peoples to stand reconciled to him. One way we can do this is by eating creatures God once prohibited. Whereas old-covenant believers *abstained* from these foods to proclaim and mirror God's holiness, new-covenant believers today can *partake* of them for the same purposes (1 Cor. 10:31). Within this framework, bacon is victory food!

## A Note on the Hebrew Roots Movement

For centuries, many Jewish followers of Christ have chosen to follow Jewish customs like eating kosher food, worshiping on Saturday, and welcoming the Sabbath with a traditional ceremony and meal. They recognize this as a free choice, not as an obligation to Moses's law or rabbinic tradition. And Paul would bless this practice, especially if the intent is to see more Jews saved (see 1 Cor. 9:20).

However, there is a growing "Hebrew Roots" movement whose primarily Gentile devotees claim Jesus's followers *need* to return to their Messiah's roots by keeping as much of the Old Testament law as possible without the temple. While they verbally affirm that justification before God is by grace alone through faith alone in Jesus alone, they teach that all believers are still *bound* to keep the Mosaic law.

Reflecting on this movement in view of Scripture, we can say that Hebrew Roots advocates are, at best, passing undue judgment on fellow believers (Rom. 14:3) and, at worst, failing to appreciate the changes that Christ brought in salvation history (Gal. 3:1–5). Whether dealing with food (2:11–14), holy days (4:10), or circumcision (5:2), all who *require* obedience to the law as if Christ has not come are seeking to "submit again to a yoke of slavery" (5:1). We cannot keep the whole law (5:3), so we must trust Christ, who has fulfilled the law for and through his elect as we live lives of love by the Spirit (Rom. 5:18; 8:3–4; 13:8–10).

## Conclusion

Because Christians are part of the new covenant and not the old, the Mosaic law bears no direct authority over believers. Nevertheless, while the New Testament authors repudiate the old Mosaic law-covenant and replace Moses's law with the law of Christ, they also reappropriate the law of Moses through Jesus. To grasp the lasting value of the old-covenant law for Christians, we must first establish the law's original meaning and application and then determine the law's theological importance, clarifying what the law teaches about God and his ways, evaluating how Christ's fulfilling the law impacts its application, and stating the love principle the law expresses.

# Conclusion

## Can Christians Really Enjoy Jesus's Bible?

*The rules of the LORD are true, and righteous altogether.*
*More to be desired are they than gold, even much fine gold;*
*sweeter also than honey and drippings from*
*the honeycomb (Ps. 19:10)*

This little book has invited you to a feast of rich food and a treasure of incomparable value. The Old Testament was Jesus's only Bible, and in it you can discover a perfect law that revives the soul, right precepts that rejoice the heart, and true rules that are altogether righteous (Ps. 19:7–9). "More to be desired are they than gold, even much fine gold; sweeter also than honey and dripping of the honeycomb" (19:10).

Through his Son's life, death, and resurrection, the reigning God eternally saves and satisfies sinners who believe and enables them to celebrate his Son's greatness through all of Scripture. And "beholding the glory of the Lord," we are "being transformed into the same image from one degree of glory to another" (2 Cor. 3:18). As a conclusion to this study, here are seven tips to those aspiring, as God intended, to delight in the Old Testament through Christ and for Christ.

# 1. Remember That the Old Testament Is **Christian** Scripture

What we call the Old Testament was the only Scripture Jesus had, and the apostles stressed that the prophets wrote God's Word to instruct Christians. Paul says, for example, that God's guidance of Israel through the wilderness was "written down for our instruction, on whom the end of the ages has come" (1 Cor. 10:11). Indeed, "whatever was written down in former days was written for our instruction, that through endurance and through the encouragement of the Scriptures we might have hope" (Rom. 15:4).

Peter emphasized that "it was revealed to them [i.e., the Old Testament prophets] that they were serving not themselves but you"—the church (1 Pet. 1:12). This means that Moses and the prophets recognized that they were writing for a future community that would be able to know, see, and hear in ways most of Israel could not (Deut. 29:4; 30:8; Isa. 29:18; 30:8; Jer. 30:1–2, 24; 31:33; Dan. 12:5–10). In short, the Old Testament is Christian Scripture that God wrote to instruct us. As Paul tells Timothy, these "sacred writings … are able to make you wise for salvation through faith in Christ Jesus," and it is this "Scripture" that is "profitable for teaching, for reproof, for correction, and for training in righteousness" (2 Tim. 3:16). *Old* in Old Testament does not mean "unimportant" or "insignificant," and we should approach the text accordingly.

# 2. Interpret the Old Testament with the Same Care You Would the New Testament

To give the same care to the Old Testament as to the New Testament means that we treat it as the very Word of God (Mark 7:13; 12:36), which Jesus considered authoritative (Matt. 4:3–4, 7, 10; 23:1–3), believed could not be broken (John 10:35), and called people to know so as to guard against doctrinal error and hell (Mark 12:24; Luke 16:28–31; 24:25; John 5:46–47). Methodologically, caring for the Old Testament means that we establish the text, consider the context, make careful observations, determine the meaning, and make relevant applications. We consider genre, literary boundaries, grammar, translation, historical and literary contexts, structure, argument flow, key words and concepts, and biblical, systematic, and practical theology.[1] We study each passage within its given book (= close context), within salvation history (= continuing context), and in relationship to Christ and the rest of Scripture (= complete context).

Many Christians will give years to understanding Mark and Romans and only weeks to Genesis, Psalms, and Isaiah, while rarely even touching the other books. When others take account of your life and ministry, may such realities not be said of you. We must consider how the Old Testament bears witness about Christ (John 5:39; cf. Luke 24:25–26, 45–47) and faithfully proclaim "the whole counsel of God" (Acts 20:27), ever doing so as those rightly handling "the word of truth" (2 Tim. 2:15).

---

1. I synthesize this approach using the acronym TCOMA: Text, Context, Observation, Meaning, Application. For each of these steps, see Jason S. DeRouchie, *Understanding and Applying Jesus's Bible: The Old Testament for Christians* (Minneapolis: Cruciform, 2025); for an expanded version, see Jason S. DeRouchie, *How to Understand and Apply the Old Testament: Twelve Steps from Exegesis to Theology* (Phillipsburg, NJ: P&R, 2017).

# 3. Treat Properly the **Covenantal** Nature of the Old Testament

The two parts of the Bible are called the Old and New Testaments because they each principally address the old and new covenants, respectively. We call Jesus's Bible a *testament* because of its covenantal quality (*testamentum* is Latin for "covenant"). The Old Testament addresses how God establishes and enforces his Mosaic covenant. And unlike the New Testament, which addresses a multinational church and was written in the common language of Greek, the Old Testament was written to Hebrews in Hebrew.

The Old Testament bears a historical particularity that requires us to observe, understand, and evaluate carefully before application. To engage the Old Testament as a *testament* requires that we recognize the distinct covenantal elements in the text and then consider how Christ's coming influences our understanding of every passage.

# 4. Remember Why the Old Testament Is Called **Old**

Building on the previous point, the Old Testament details the Mosaic covenant of which Christians are not a part and that has been superseded by the new (Jer. 31:31–34). This fact requires that Christians carefully consider how Christ fulfills every Old Testament story, promise, and law before establishing its relevance. Indeed, all history (Mark 1:14), every promise (2 Cor. 1:20), and the entire law-covenant (Rom. 10:4) point to him. While Moses's instructions still have value for Christians, they do so only through Christ (Deut. 30:8; Matt. 5:17–19). Similarly, while every promise is Yes for Christians, it is so only in Jesus (2 Cor. 1:20). He is the seed of Abraham (Gal. 1:16), and we become Abraham's offspring only in Christ (3:29).

As Christians, we must interpret the Old Testament in view of Jesus's coming. His person and work realize what the Old Testament anticipates (Matt. 5:17–18; Luke 24:44; Acts 3:18), he stands as the substance of all Old Testament shadows (Col. 2:16–17), and he embodies every ethical ideal found in both the law and wisdom (Rom. 5:18–19; 1 Cor. 1:30). We need to recognize that one of the Old Testament's fundamental purposes is to help us celebrate Christ and all God would accomplish through him. We must consider God's whole counsel (Acts 20:27) in relation to the cross (1 Cor. 2:2).

# 5. Read the Old Testament through the Light and Lens of Christ

Jesus supplies both the light and lens for reading the Old Testament rightly. "Light" indicates that interpreting the Old Testament properly is possible only for those who have seen "the light of the gospel of the glory of Christ" (2 Cor. 4:4). Only spiritual people can read a spiritual book (1 Cor. 2:13–14). "Lens" stresses that Jesus's life, death, and resurrection disclose truths in the Old Testament that were always there but not yet clear, at least to the majority (Rom. 16:25–26; 2 Cor. 3:14). Christians must recognize that there are significant continuities between the Testaments, such that many righteous people saw Christ from a distance (Matt. 13:17; Luke 10:24; John 8:56; 1 Pet. 1:10–12). On the other hand, there are also significant discontinuities, in that the rebel population was not given a heart to understand (Deut. 29:4; Isa. 6:9–10), nor did God disclose the mystery of the kingdom until Christ came (Dan. 12:8–10; Mark 4:11–12; cf. Eph. 3:5).

The New Testament provides both the answer key and the algorithm for reading the Old Testament in its fullness. By elevating Christ's person and work, the New Testament signals the substance of all previous shadows, realizes the hopes of all previous anticipations, and clarifies how the various Old Testament patterns and trajectories find their resolve. Through Jesus, God enables and empowers us to read the Old Testament as he intended. Jesus is both our light and lens, and we read the Old Testament rightly only through Christ and for Christ.

# 6. Consider How Faithfully to See and Celebrate Christ in the Old Testament

Christians must seek to analyze and synthesize how the whole Bible progresses, integrates, and climaxes in Christ. As noted in chapter two, following the lead of Scripture itself, we can see and celebrate Christ from the Old Testament in numerous ways.

1. Consider how Christ stands as the climax of the redemptive story.

2. Identify how Christ fulfills messianic predictions.

3. Recognize how Christ's coming creates numerous similarities and contrasts between the old and new ages, creations, and covenants.

4. Determine how Christ is the antitype to Old Testament types.

5. Reflect on how Yahweh's person and work anticipates Christ.

6. Contemplate how Christ embodies every ethical ideal from Old Testament law and wisdom.

7. Instruct from the Old Testament through Christ's mediation—both through the pardon he supplies, which secures both promises and power, and the pattern of godliness that he sets.

# 7. Assess How the New Testament Authors Are Using the Old Testament

The early church devoted itself to the apostles' teaching (Acts 2:42), and the whole church is built on the foundation of the apostles and prophets, with Jesus as the cornerstone (Eph. 2:20). Yet what Bible were the apostles using? They were using the Old Testament, and they were making much of Christ from it. As Luke tells us regarding Paul's ministry in Rome: "From morning till evening he expounded to them, testifying to the kingdom of God and trying to convince them about Jesus both from the Law of Moses and from the Prophets" (Acts 28:23). The New Testament is loaded with quotations of and allusions to the Old Testament, and we should note the significance of these citations.

When Paul asserted to the Corinthians, "I decided to know nothing among you except Jesus Christ and him crucified" (1 Cor. 2:2), he did so as an Old Testament preacher. And when he claimed that "all Scripture ... is profitable" (2 Tim. 3:16), the "Scripture" he principally had in mind was the Old Testament, which is "able to make you wise for salvation through faith in Christ Jesus" (3:15). You will help yourself and your people to cherish the whole counsel of God (Acts 20:27) and to appreciate the whole Bible when you take the time to wrestle with the New Testament's citations of the Old.

## Conclusion

The Old Testament is Christian Scripture, and we can delight in it best when we approach it through Christ and for Christ. The Old Testament magnifies Jesus in numerous ways, and his person and work clarify how to discern rightly the continuities and discontinuities of salvation history. Through the light and lens that Christ supplies, Christians can enjoy the same God and the same good news in both Testaments. We can also embrace all God's promises and rightly apply Moses's law as revelation, prophecy, and wisdom.

The Old Testament is for Christians. Start enjoying Jesus's Bible through Christ and for Christ!

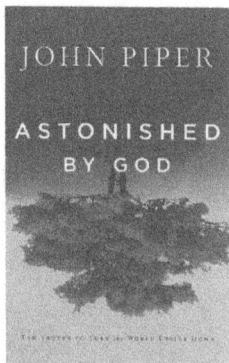

## Astonished by God
### Ten Truths to Turn the World Upside Down

John Piper | 192 pages

*Turn your world on its head.*

**bit.ly/AstonishedbyGod**

## The Joy Project:
### An Introduction to Calvinism
### (with Study Guide)

Tony Reinke
Foreword by John Piper | 168 pages

*True happiness isn't found. It finds you.*

**bit.ly/JOYPROJECT**

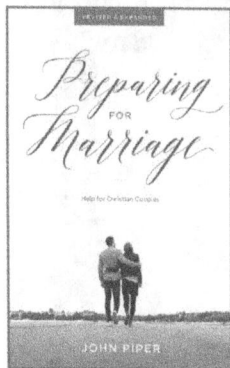


## Preparing for Marriage
### Help for Christian Couples

John Piper | 86 pages

*As you prepare for marriage, dare to dream with God.*

**bit.ly/prep-for-marriage**

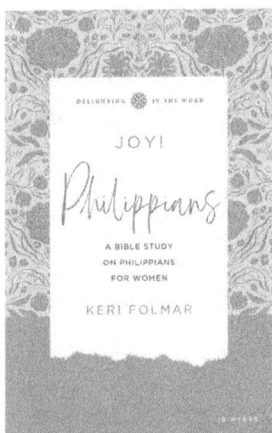 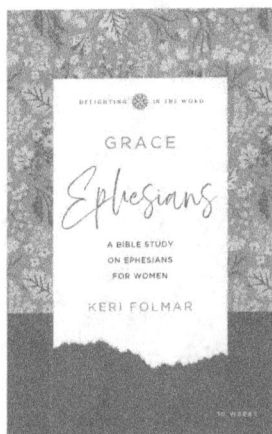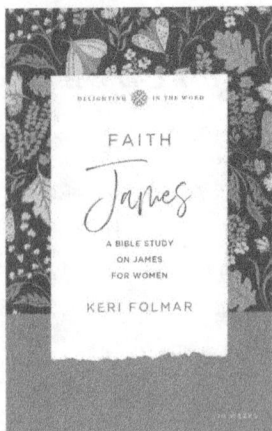 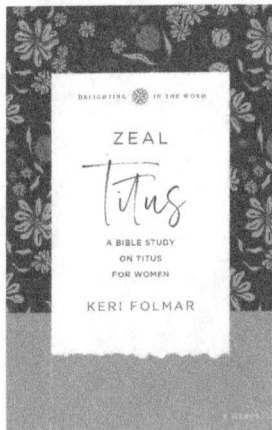

DELIGHTING IN THE WORD

*Keri Folmar's fully inductive Bible studies for women are ideal for personal use, groups, or one-on-one mentoring. Spiral-bound for ease of use, the Delighting in the Word studies have plenty of room to write and take notes. Each multi-week study (five days per week) covers an entire book of the Bible, guiding you deeper into God's word through wise, helpful, and illuminating questions that enable you to Observe, Interpret, and Apply Scripture to your life.*

Vol. 1
18 weeks

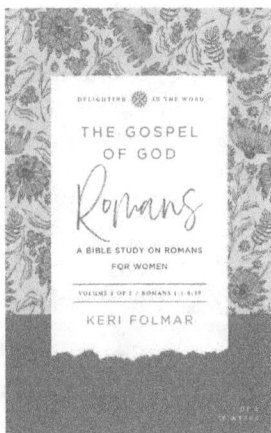

Vol. 2
18 weeks

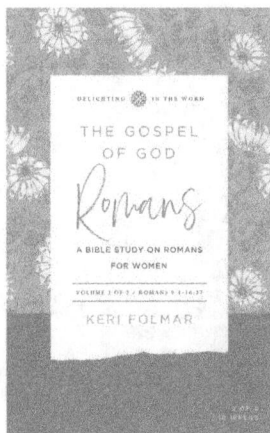

Vol. 1
11 weeks

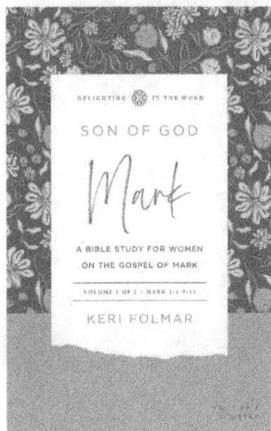

Vol. 2
11 weeks

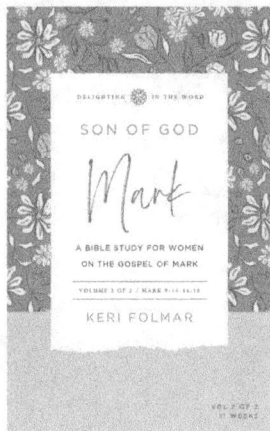

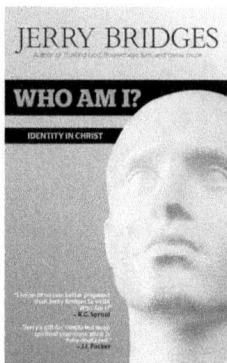

## Who Am I?
### Identity in Christ

Jerry Bridges | 91 pages

*Jerry Bridges unpacks Scripture to give the Christian eight clear, simple, interlocking answers to one of the most essential questions of life.*

**bit.ly/WHOAMI**

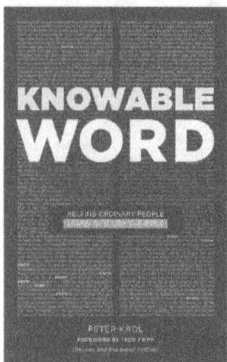

Two books by Peter Krol

**Knowable Word**
*Helping Ordinary People Learn to Study the Bible (Revised and Expanded)*
bit.ly/Knowable

**Sowable Word**
*Helping Ordinary People Learn to Lead Bible Studies*
bit.ly/Sowable

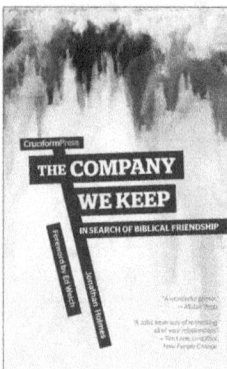

## The Company We Keep
### In Search of Biblical Friendship

Jonathan Holmes
Foreword by Ed Welch | 112 pages

*Biblical friendship is deep, honest, pure, tranparent, and liberating. It is also attainable.*

**bit.ly/B-Friend**

www.ingramcontent.com/pod-product-compliance
Lightning Source LLC
LaVergne TN
LVHW052031080426
835513LV00018B/2274